THRILLER

The Movie Treasury

MOVIES

Classic Films of Suspense and Mystery

Lawrence Hammond

OCTOPUS
OCTOPUS BOOKS

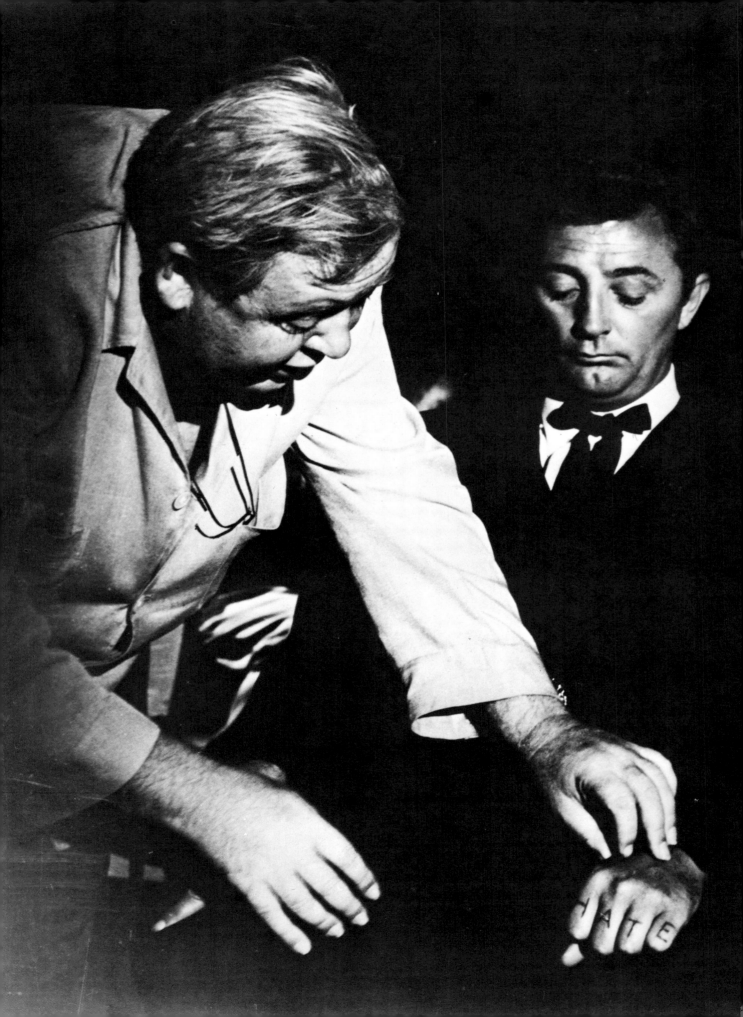

Contents

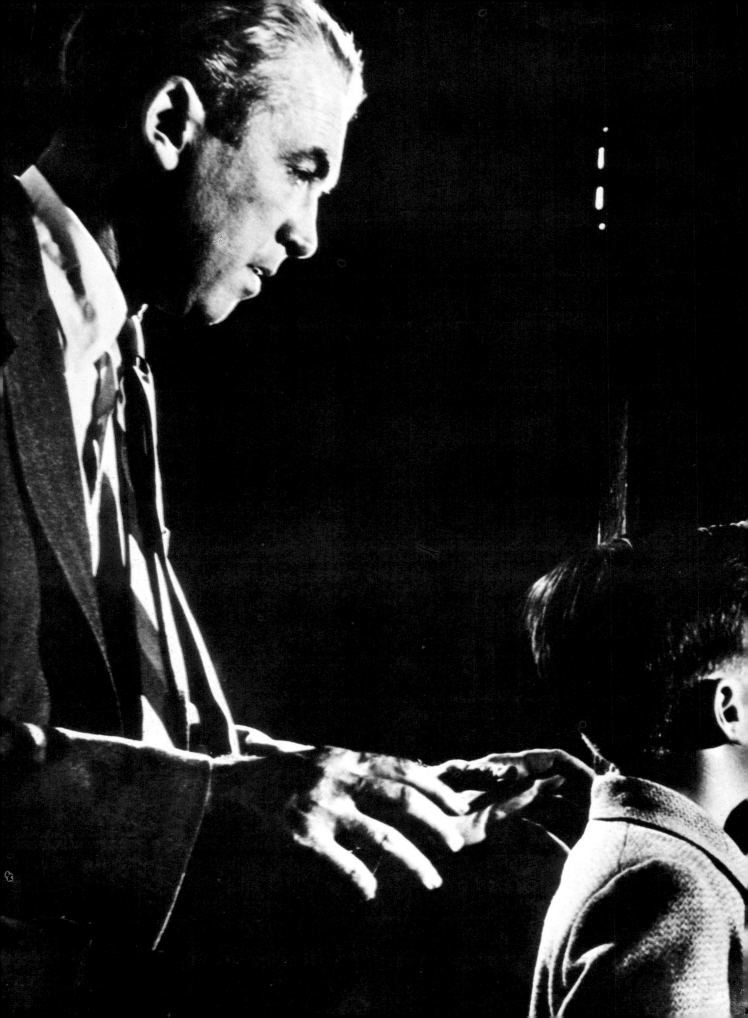

Moments of Menace

*Suspense is a fatherly James Stewart
(preceding pages) on the track of*
The Man Who Knew Too Much
*(Paramount-Filwite 1955) . . . or
Humphrey Bogart as the classic private
eye (above) in* The Big Sleep *(WB 1946)
. . . it can be the threatening figure in the
doorway (right) in* Wait Until Dark
*(WB-Seven Arts 1967) . . . or Albert
Finney (overleaf) in* Gumshoe
(Memorial 1971)

"THIS suspense," the man said, "is terrible. I hope it will last."

The man was Oscar Wilde, and there was too much suspense in his life to leave room for it in his art. But the reaction is true, and has been throughout the eons of recorded history since man was first able to pause long enough from the urgent business of staying alive to feel the need for escape. The escape that worked best in pulling him gently by the hand (or sometimes jerking him by the hair) from the tensions and dangers of the real world was that which created the tensions and dangers of an imaginary world. The higher the pitch of tension created by the artist, the nearer it could get to intolerable suspense, the more effective it was in enthralling the reader or watcher. "The suspense is killing me – and I like it!"

This, of course, is the secret that has always been known to the storytellers of this world. Storytellers using tools other than the written word, too. A famous playwright once advised me: "If you can't write your actors into a crisis of suspense – however minor – every three minutes, then tear it up." And of all the media that can be used for telling a story, none has yet been invented with the power, the range, the flexibility, the scope of multi-dimensional assault on the emotions to match that of the cinema. This is why I believe there is no form of storytelling so potentially effective as the suspense film.

It is not the horror film; it is not (necessarily) the film of violence. Anyone who has ever edged towards the front of that upholstered seat, who has unconsciously reached out a hand to seek a consoling grip on the hand of a companion when the tension flitting across the screen became unbearable – that cinemagoer knows what a suspense film is. It is not true to say that when you have seen one you have seen them all. But it is true that when you have seen one you want to see a thousand more, and you do not need any definition.

In fact, a thesis could be written (and doubtless has been) to define the suspense movie; and the very academic possibility defines its irrelevance.

As I think back over 35 years of film-watching, it is not the artistic integrity, the social relevance, the philosophic values or any other of the clichés abstracted from refined air by refined critics that I remember. It is not the jumpcuts, the dolly shots, the quick "pans" or the slow fades or any other of the technical jargon. It is not even the frantic scrambles of some producers to try to raise another fifty thousand dollars by tonight to pay to finish shooting the movie; nor a scriptwriter coolly

LEFT *Frank Sinatra, with not a song in sight, was mixed up with espionage in postwar ruined Germany in* The Naked Runner *(Artanis Enterprises 1967)*
ABOVE *Humphrey Bogart in another scene from* The Big Sleep *(WB 1946)*

writing scene 87 behind the cameras and rushing it off, page by page, to be typed while scene 86 was still being shot.

It is not skeletons and skulls and beetles crawling from empty eye-sockets; nor is it blood and guts pouring from mutilated bodies; nor again multiple rape clinically contrived for maximum titillation of a jaded audience.

As I look down at the typewriter keys, they slowly dissolve and I see a montage: a tiny silhouetted figure bisected by the crossed hairlines of a telescopic sight . . . a shadow across a hallway . . . a closed door, innocent except that I'm scared stiff to know who will walk through it . . . a bunch of chatelaine keys hanging by the black bombazine skirts of a grim housekeeper . . . two figures argu-

ing murderously through the windows of a neighbouring apartment, so near yet unapproachably distant.

I look over the edge of a vertiginous cliff, and up the clanging black treads of a seemingly never-ending fire escape. I hear the clacking of a pursuing helicopter, like some monstrous winged beetle, swooping low and lethal over the land, and there is nowhere for me to hide . . . I am a tiny figure, hanging like a fly from the huge sculpted face of an American President on Mount Rushmore . . . and I'm Humphrey Bogart and I light a casual cigarette while my eyes are like gimlets, and I thrust a hand into my raincoat pocket and say through the smoke: "Take it easy fellas and nobody's gonna get hurt" . . .

13

All this I see, and I know then what a suspense movie is without any academic definition, and I see so much more. I see a gun sliding round a stark and shadowed column in a whole colonnade of them in Paris, and it barks its deadly shot at me, but I'm OK, darling, because I'm Cary Grant, and I can also nip across the rooftops like a cat, while you hold your breath . . . I see many a rooftop, and many a hunter and hunted over them, and many a high-up ledge with a guy or a girl hanging on by the fingernails, because you know and I know that there's an extra element of danger and, therefore, of suspense if I can so easily fall to my death even if I escape the heavies hot on my heels.

And those stairs: so many stairs, climbing ever upwards, sometimes spiralling, because they can shoot up at me through them, and you know and maybe I don't yet know – but I will, I will – that when I get to the top there'll be nowhere else to go and there'll be death in front of me and death behind me . . . till the last reel.

I see this man hanging by his fingertips from the guttering of a roof high above the teeming, heedless city, and by now they're my fingertips, and this other guy is grinding his foot on them, and I don't know how long I can hold on, and the guttering is beginning to break away . . . Or maybe it's not a roof, it's a clifftop, and it's starting to crumble, but still his foot is grinding my aching fingers, and

Moments of Menace spanning 30 years;
LEFT *Fritz Lang's* M *(Lang-Nero Film 1931)*
TOP RIGHT *James Stewart fights for his life in* The Man Who Knew Too Much *(Paramount-Filwite 1955)*
RIGHT *The anguished eyes of Anthony Perkins in Alfred Hitchcock's* Psycho *(Shamley 1960)*

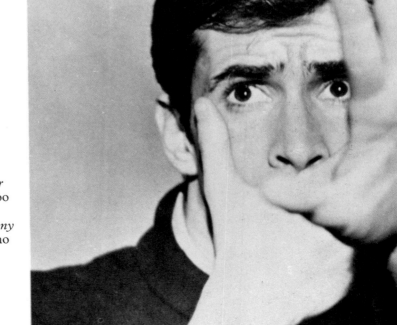

can I? Can I summon the strength to grab his ankle and give it a jerk, and will he hurtle to his death, or will we both go down? Or will he stumble into the great illuminated sign that flashes on and off and adds so powerfully to the tension built into the very lighting of the film, and will that (to the total surprise of everyone except the producer, director, screenwriter, technicians and cast) electrocute him and save me in the 98th minute?

Ah, those flashing illuminated signs – now on, luridly lighting the sleazy little office with the filing cabinet that has nothing but my quart of Scotch in it, the hatstand where (after careful practice) I can hook my snap-brim by tossing it airily across the room, the desk which I use to prop my feet; now it's off, and in the shadowed semi-darkness you can just see the glowing tip of my cigarette and the dull sheen of my Police Special .38 or maybe my .45 or my Luger as I check its action and slip it into the drawer, which I carefully leave half-open; and the only other light comes from the hallway through my glass office door on which, if you can make out the reversed lettering, you can read: "Private detective". And the sign flashes on again and through that door comes a dame, and she's well-stacked and well-heeled and she says in an educated kinda voice: "Mr Marlowe? I have a case I'd like you to investigate," and I say, leaving

Two famous scenes from Hitchcock's North by Northwest *(MGM 1959);*
Cary Grant pursued by a crop-dusting plane (above) *and trapped with*
Eva Marie-Saint (below)

my feet where they are: "Sure I'm Philip Marlowe" . . . and we're off into *The Big Sleep* or *The Lady in the Lake*. Or maybe I'm not Marlowe this time. Maybe I'm Sam Spade, but the office and the Scotch and the hatstand and the gun – and my feet – are still the same and we're off into an equal sometime-never-land of laconic suspense with *The Maltese Falcon* or *The Glass Key*.

I hear the mournful hoot of a ship's siren, sounding threatening through the swirling fog; and I hear the sound of a thousand birds turned killers. I hear the creak of a floorboard under an alien foot. I see a young man, a mother's son, with madness and murder in his eyes, walking purposefully up a harmless staircase, narrowed into menace by perspective; and I see a doorknob turn and I know, my God I know, whose hand is doing it. I see a disembodied waxworks hand, and I see a dead hand lolling from a sack of potatoes, and I see a hand smashing (it seems) straight into the camera, which is my face, and everything goes dark. Or blood red.

I see a great wheel turning musically in a fairground, and I'm at the top of it, hunted and confident and not yet cracking; and I see an echoing sewer beneath the city and panic and pursuit are there. I see a waxworks crammed with still figures, in the half-light, but one of them isn't wax: one of them is human and intends to kill me. I see a hall of mirrors, and he's there and she's there, and they each have a gun, and they are reflected a thousand thousand times in the myriad images, and which is the reality and which the reflection? And the guns fire and the mirrors shatter until one of the images doesn't shatter into splintered glass, but sinks to the floor, and that was the reality (and almost the end of the film).

I see a showerbath, and a pool of something that isn't water, spreading, spreading . . .

Those are the things this book is about. Those sorts of things, and some of the people who created them. This is not an academic book, nor a catalogue or encyclopedia. It is a personal book about the suspense movies that haunt him, written by a man who has never been able to resist them. And it is written for people bitten by the same bug – which means anyone who has ever seen a good movie.

Before we go on: Do you recognise any of the scenes mentioned in this chapter? They are moments from classic suspense films, some of my thriller-favourites. This is a private competition, and there is a private prize: If you do recognise them, maybe they will recall to you some of those films which have given so much pleasure to so many by creating unforgettable moments of menace in their session of suspense.

BELOW *Robert Mitchum, as the crazed preacher, meets a sticky end in* The Night of the Hunter *(Gregory 1955)*

Learning
the Rules

SUSPENSE, in the simplest terms of compelling us to wonder what is coming next, is of the essence of story-telling, and the men who forged the young crafty art of the cinema knew this instinctively. The first "fiction" film of which I can find record – Louis Lumière's *L'Arroseur Arrosé*, which flickered into history in 1895 – featured a gardener peering down the nozzle of a hose and wondering why it was not working. The audience knew the reason was that a boy was standing on the hose. Instant suspense – will he, won't he, when will he? – until the boy moves off and the water jets out and hits the gardener.

In that primitive moment Lumière hit upon the first rule of suspense: tell the audience all the facts. If we had not seen the boy standing on the hose,

what to expect," said Hitchcock, "the audience wait for it to happen. This conditioning of the viewer is essential to the build-up of suspense."

The infant film industries of Europe and the United States were quick to jump on the suspense bandwagon: indeed, to our more sophisticated eyes, suspense seems to have been virtually the only ingredient, apart from movement, of those early cliff-hangers. The camera work was as crude as the voiceless acting; the characterisations simplified to caricature. But a suspenseful story was what they had to sell, and they fast learned how to tell it.

Those were the breathless years, in the first decade of the century, when a movie was shot in a couple of days: in New York in the summer when the weather was good; then, when winter came and

PRECEDING PAGES *The make-up was heavy, the acting even heavier but the audiences flocked to D. W. Griffith's* The Lonedale Operator *(Biograph 1911)*
The cinema was an early learner of the rules of suspense;
LEFT *Louis Lumière's* L'Arroseur Arrosé *(1895)*
RIGHT *A D. W. Griffith's thriller from 1908*

there might have been surprise when the gardener got the water in the face, but no suspense. The suspense was built because we knew more than the gardener; we were wondering when and how it would happen, and what the main characters' reactions would be.

It is interesting that this has always been a prime rule of the man who has made more and better suspense films than anyone else in the history of the cinema, the man who is unquestionably the master of suspense: Alfred Hitchcock. Seventy years after Lumière's film, Hitchcock was emphasising to the young French film director François Truffaut the importance of providing the audience with all the facts of a situation, including information the other characters in the movie don't know. "Knowing

the light changed, out by train across the American continent to California to catch the sun.

D. W. Griffith, the pioneer of the film as we know it today, made more than 400 one-reel and two-reel movies in five years. He set the pattern of these simple, direct and suspenseful stories right from the start. The first film Griffith directed – in July 1908 – was *The Adventures of Dollie*. He showed a gypsy snatching a woman's purse and getting whipped by the husband as punishment. The gypsy seizes their child Dollie in revenge, carries her off to his camp where he gags her and hides her in a water barrel. Later, as the gypsy is fording a stream, the barrel falls off his wagon into the water and is carried away by the current. We see the barrel, with hapless Dollie inside, bobbing downstream towards

THE ADVENTURES OF DOLLIE

HER MARVELOUS EXPERIENCE AT THE HANDS OF GYPSIES

LENGTH, 713 FEET.   PRICE, 14 CENTS PER FOOT.

One of the most remarkable cases of child-stealing is depicted in this Biograph picture, showing the thwarting by a kind Providence of the attempt to kidnap for revenge a pretty little girl by a Gypsy. On the lawn of a country residence we find the little family, comprising father, mother and little Dollie, their daughter. In front of the grounds there flows a picturesque stream to which the mother and little one go to watch the boys fishing. There has come into the neighborhood a band of those peripatetic Nomads of the Zingani type, whose ostensible occupation is selling baskets and reed ware, but their real motive is pillage. While the mother and child are seated on the wall beside the stream, one of these Gypsies approaches and offers for sale several baskets. A refusal raises his ire and he seizes the woman's purse and is about to make off with it when the husband, hearing her cries of alarm, rushes down to her aid, and with a heavy snakewhip lashes the Gypsy unmercifully, leaving great welts upon his swarthy body, at the same time arousing the venom of his black heart. The Gypsy leaves the scene vowing vengeance, and the little family go, back to the lawn, where the father amuses little Dollie with a game of battledore and shuttlecock. During the game the mother calls papa to the house for an instant. This is the Gypsy's chance, for he has been hiding in the bushes all the while. He seizes the child and carries her to his camp where he gags and conceals her in a watercask. A search of the Gypsy's effects by the distracted father proves fruitless and the Gypsy with the aid of his wife gathers up his traps into his wagon, placing the cask containing the child on the back. Down the road they go at breakneck speed, and as they ford a stream the cask falls off the wagon into the water and is carried away by the current. Next we see the cask floating down the stream toward a waterfall, over which it goes; then through the seething spray of the rapids, and on, on until it finally enters the quiet cove of the first scene, where it is brought ashore by the fisherboys. Hearing strange sounds emitted from the barrel, the boys call for the bereft father, who is still searching for the lost one. Breaking the head from the barrel the amazed and happy parents now fold in their arms their loved one, who is not much worse off for her marvelous experience.

No. 3454   CODE WORD--Reverso

Produced and Controlled Exclusively by the
American Mutoscope & Biograph Co.
11 East 14th Street, New York City

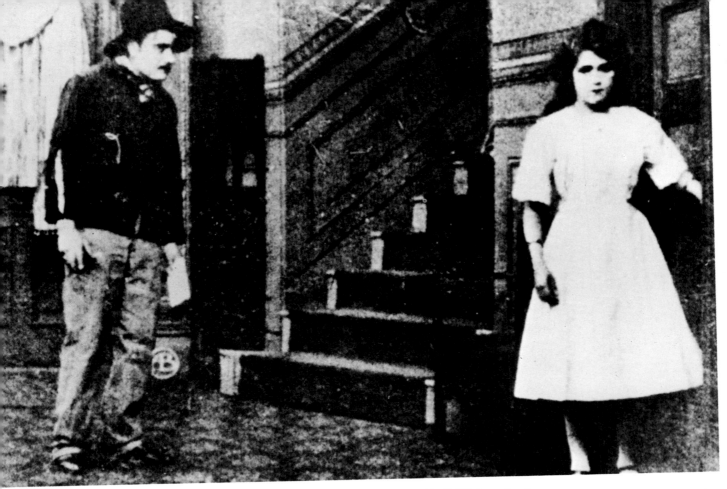

ABOVE & BELOW *A couple of days were enough for D. W. Griffith to shoot a film like* The Lonely Villa *(Biograph 1909)*
OPPOSITE *The pioneer director on the set*

E LONELY VIL

e is something spooklike in the title of this Biograph subj
ay that the incidents are of a decidedly material nature, and
to be most intensely thrilling, gripping the spectator from sta
Cullison resides in a very beautiful country villa, far rer
neighbors, and about twenty miles from the city   He is expec
other, who is to arrive in the city from the West the next mor
is learn by a couple of crooks, who plan to get Cullison away
him a fake letter by an apparently idiotic country bumpkin w
Have taken an earlier train. Will arrive in New York 10 30 P
r Mother "   He gets ready, as it is now nearly eight o'clock
g adieu to his wife and three young children, the bumpkin is
nder the prete se of dozing in the doorway   Realizing h

a weir, over it and through the seething rapids, until finally it is washed ashore at the cove where the film started. Some boys hear sounds from inside the barrel, summon the father who is still searching for his lost daughter – and there, inside the barrel, he discovers his Dollie, none the worse for wear.

Don't laugh. Griffith made his film in two days. And what do you expect for that? *War and Peace*?

Films like this brought the thrill of vicarious excitement to millions, and set a pattern of story-telling on which an entire industry of universal entertainment was built.

Griffith hated to use a script – in direct contrast to the methods of Hitchcock, who represents the distillation of all the lessons the cinema has learned in 60 years of suspense movies. Hitchcock not only works painstakingly on the scripts with his writers, occasionally to their despair ("If you can puzzle it out yourself, what do you need me for?" asked Raymond Chandler when they were failing to see eye-to-eye on the script of *Strangers on a Train*): before shooting starts, he has every last detail of his

films worked out in advance, every camera angle, every shot, every line, every point of dress and of décor, every last nuance of acting.

Much had to be learned before such professionalism could be exercised; and most of what has been learned has come from D. W. Griffith. This one-time small-part actor and aspiring and unsuccessful playwright revolutionised the craft of storytelling on the screen and in so doing developed the techniques which makers of suspense movies have used ever since. It has been said with truth that, after Griffith, nothing new was added to the film.

When he began, a film was made entirely in medium shot from a single immobile camera set up to photograph the actors in full-length view. It was Griffith who realised that suspense (and therefore storytelling) demanded drawing the audience into the action, compelling the public on the hard seats to feel involved and identified with the actors. He

reinvented the close-up for the commercial cinema (a man called George Albert Smith had used close-ups as early as 1900) . . . and, like all pioneers, Griffith was at first derided. "When I first photographed players at close range," he said later, "my management and patrons decried a method that showed only the face of the story characters . . . Today" (he was speaking in 1921) "the close-up is employed by nearly all directors to bring a picture audience to an intimate acquaintance with an actor's emotions."

Before Griffith, film stories were told by the alphabet technique – they started at A and (once the novelty of the medium had worn off) yawned through to Z in a straightforward time sequence. He devised flashbacks. In the same interview in 1921 he said: "I adopted the flashback to build suspense, which until then had been a missing quality in picture dramas. Instead of showing a continuous view of a girl floating downstream in a barrel, I cut into the film by flashing back to incidents that contributed to the scene and explained it."

While he was pioneering the development of lighting effects and tight editing in American films, Griffith was discovering the benefits of cross-cutting from scene to scene to heighten tension. As early as 1909, in *The Lonely Villa*, he cross-cut scenes of a mother shielding her child from some villains with shots of the father speeding to the rescue.

At first, the cross-cutting techniques were used only in the inevitable chases, flashing from pursued to pursuers. Griffith refined and strengthened the technique so that it was used through the whole film.

An example that's hard to beat was in 1911 with a thriller called *The Lonedale Operator*. It was the story of a beautiful railway telegrapher saved, at the last minute, from some tramps bent on theft. To build up his suspense Griffith intercut shots of the girl, Blanche Sweet, trying to call help with shots of the tramps trying to break into her office, and with shots of a train crew speeding to the rescue. Each scene was cut shorter and shorter, speeding the tempo, until, at the crucial moments when the girl was really at bay, Griffith suddenly extended the train sequence, holding the suspense to breaking-point before quickly ending with the rescue. Not a second was wasted on unnecessary detail . . . another precursor of the Hitchcock belief that "drama is life with the dull bits cut out."

By 1912 Griffith had developed practically the whole armoury of suspense-building techniques

LEFT *The railroad was a popular ingredient in Griffith's formula of suspense and action in* The Girl and Her Trust *(Biograph 1912)*
ABOVE *The director, who was also a master editor, checking yet another reel*

which directors have employed ever since. He was not only getting extra punch from close-ups, extra tension from editing, cross-cutting scenes and shots, extra atmosphere from using more back-lighting, introducing long shots for scenery, mixing medium and close shots, composing his actors into diagonal movements across the frame: he was now using multiple cameras for the first time and increasingly using a moving camera mounted on a train.

When he remade *The Lonedale Operator* as *The Girl and Her Trust*, with Dorothy Bernard, his camerawork was infinitely more sophisticated and, as a result, the suspense exerted a stronger grip. This time he mounted a camera on a railway hand-car and intercut shots from that with shots of the pursuing locomotive made from fixed cameras. Then he intercut shots taken from a car travelling parallel to both handcar and locomotive – "tracking shots". There was the same breathless editing of shorter and shorter shots, bringing the handcar and the locomotive closer and closer without showing them in the same shot . . . until the last shot showed the train catching up from the rear.

Of course, the new audiences flocking in their millions to the new entertainment were unaware of these techniques as such. All they knew was that films had become more exciting and suspense had come to the cinema.

M for Murder

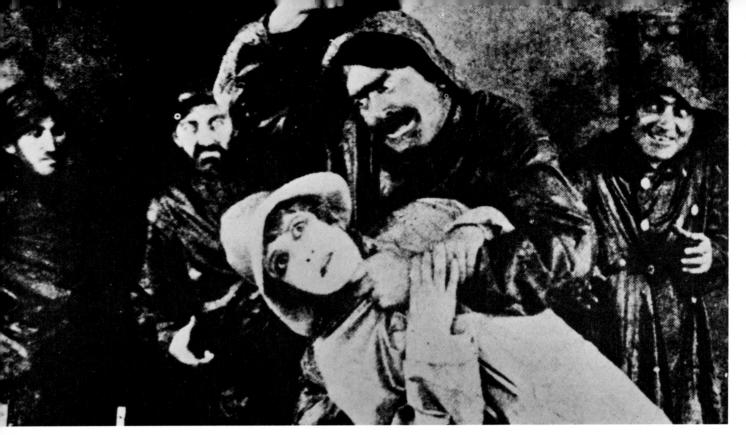

PRECEDING PAGES *Cornered. A blind beggar blocks Peter Lorre's escape in*
M *(Lang-Nero Film 1931)*
ABOVE *Early serials like* The Perils of Pauline *(Eclectic Films for Pathe*
1914) brought a new concept to the movies: "The Cliff-hanger" and Harold
Lloyd (below), teetering hazardously, brought it to a fine art in Safety Last
(Roach 1923)
RIGHT *Audrey Hepburn clutching the heroin stuffed doll in* Wait Until Dark
(WB-Seven Arts 1967)
OVERLEAF *The Collector (The Collector Co. 1965) and what Terence*
Stamp collected was Samantha Eggar

WHILE D. W. Griffith went on to construct such massive milestones in the commercial cinema as *The Birth of a Nation, Intolerance, Broken Blossoms,* an army of emulators applied the lessons of his techniques to turning out the thousands of films that were needed to keep the audiences on the edge of their seats in the mushrooming new cinemas.

Suspense preoccupied them . . . in the eternal chase sequences of elemental Hollywood, the cliff-hanging serials like *The Perils of Pauline* in 1914 and *The Exploits of Elaine* in 1915, which kept audiences on tenterhooks from week to week.

Alongside the suspense that was rooted in fear, was the suspense that became allied to comedy. Recall, for a moment, the perennial ledge-hanging antics of Harold Lloyd, dangling heart-stoppingly (even if you didn't know he was not using a double or any trick effects) by one hand high above the street; antics which put a catch in the throat of laughter and chilled the comedy element for some people while heightening the release of the next guffaw.

28

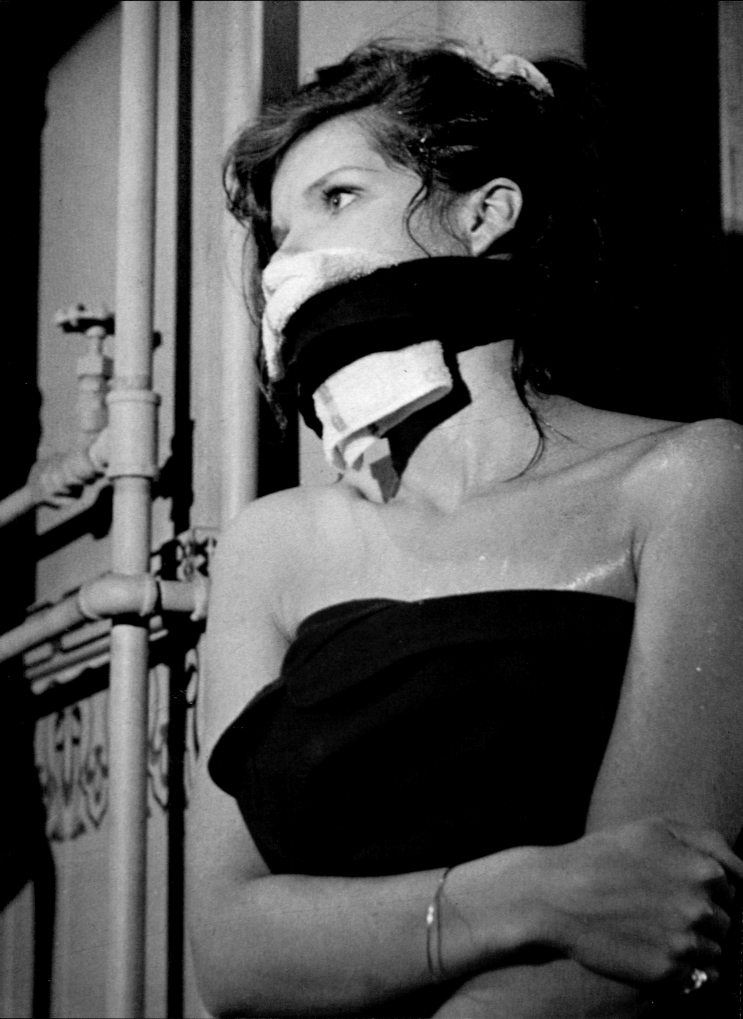

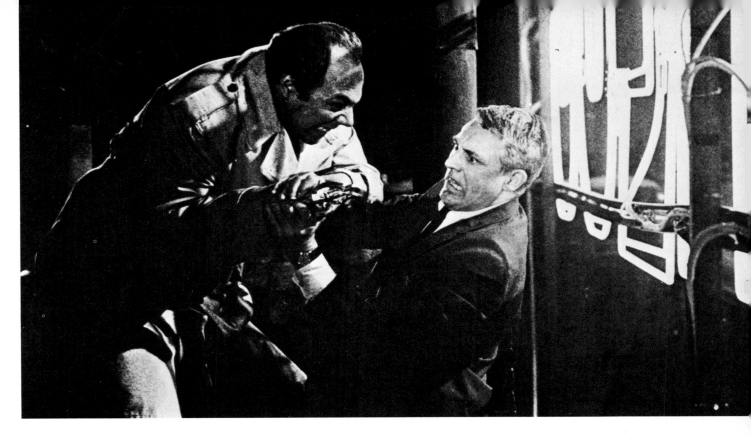

The movies have always been an industry which, to put it politely, considered that a really good idea was something which was far too precious to use only once.

Compare Harold Lloyd hanging fearsomely from any of his ledges with, say, Cary Grant holding his life in his fingertips as he hung from the guttering of a Parisian roof in Stanley Donen's *Charade* (1963); or the same carefree charmer hanging with Eva-Marie Saint like a fly from the huge stone face of a US President carved on Mount Rushmore in Hitchcock's *North by Northwest* (1959) – and keeping his cool sufficiently to chat wittily to the blonde about his previous marriages. Compare the car chases of a score of Keystone Cops or Laurel and Hardy comedies with the suspense-on-four-wheels highspot of, say, *Bullitt* (1968). And even Monsieur Lumière's sight-gag with the hose has had them rolling in the aisles more times than one can count.

LEFT *Menace casts a shadow on Audrey Hepburn in* Wait Until Dark *(WB-Seven Arts 1967) Cary Grant always rises to the occasion (and nearly falls off it!) . . . on a rooftop above Paris (above) in* Charade *(Stanley Doners 1963) . . . and (right) on Mount Rushmore in* North by Northwest *(MGM 1959)*

For all their popularity, the serials were little more than animated strip-cartoons, as ephemeral as their own climaxes, made to be forgotten as soon as the next instalment, or the next serial, came along. The United States was not alone in this pioneer field. The Italians and the Russians were filming costume "spectaculars" in 1912–13. Before 1914, the French Pathé company alone, which introduced the cliff-hanging weekly serials to the USA, was distributing twice as much film in North America as the entire American industry. In Germany, a rapidly-growing film industry was turning out not only serials, but heavy melodramas of two, three or even up to eight instalments, each instalment of feature length. And among the Berlin talent, first scripting, then as an assistant director, and finally directing was a man who was to become one of the cinema's notable proponents of suspense: Fritz Lang.

Few of his early silent films survive, but it is interesting to observe that, by all accounts, one of his recurring themes was that of a beautiful woman enslaving a man by love. This was the theme to which he returned in one of his most successful Hollywood films, *The Woman in the Window*, in 1944. Crime melodrama featured heavily in his work; and an idea which became an early landmark in thriller movies: the mastermind of crime.

This idea found its earliest expression in 1922 in *Dr Mabuse, der Spieler (Dr Mabuse, the Gambler)* a melodrama in two episodes, running altogether about $4\frac{1}{2}$ hours, about a warped genius with a mania for power who runs a secret organisation of murderers, thieves and forgers. Mabuse, played by Rudolf Klein-Rogge, was a man of many disguises; he was also a psychiatrist; and he wielded his power by a hypnotism which to our eyes is much funnier than it was meant to be: a twitch of an eyebrow and a hard stare were enough to make the victim carry out the evil doctor's commands. Either Lang did not know or did not care then what Griffith had been doing in America, but there is little evidence in *Mabuse* of the editing and intercutting techniques which would have heightened the tensions of the action-filled plot. Even the principal car chase seemed to plod on from A to Z without intercutting.

But *Mabuse* had some good suspense ideas which have clearly influenced later generations of directors: Mabuse in a box at the Folies Bergères hypnotising a young millionaire; the investigator almost hypnotised in a card game, then gassed in a car, later hypnotised at a public show (by Mabuse in disguise) into committing suicide by driving his

34

car into a quarry. The investigator is saved, leads the police in a mass attack on the headquarters of Mabuse, who flees through the sewers (Harry Lime, where are you now?) to his counterfeiters' workshop, where he plays a game of cards with the ghosts of his victims, loses, hurls the counterfeit money in the air and lets himself be arrested – quite insane – and taken off to the asylum.

In 1932 Lang returned to the same character and theme with a new film called *Das Testament des Dr Mabuse* (*The Last Will of Dr Mabuse*) with the same actor playing the title role. For all its excitement, action, fantasy, this film would for me live in the history of the cinema just for one short scene. It deals with a killing at traffic lights as a driver is shot from a car that has pulled alongside his, the sound of the shot obliterated by the hooting of the horns of the other impatient motorists. But Lang never takes us right *into* the incident. At the payoff we look down from an overhead angle on the cars packed together at the signals: then they all pull away – all but one, which remains motionless and alone in the middle of the road after the lights have changed. No violence, no blood, is needed for us to be eerily aware that a man who was alive when the lights were at red is dead now they are at green.

Between the two Mabuse films Lang was responsible for several other German productions including the almost unbelievable *Metropolis*. It has nothing much to do with suspense (beyond the fact that once again it contains an omnipotent leader), but it was such an epoch-making movie that no mention of Lang's name can be made without it. This science fiction fantasy, set in the year 2000, was the most expensive and ambitious picture made in Europe up to that time. It took 310 days to shoot in 1925–26; exposed nearly two million feet of film; used more than 36,000 men, women and children in its cast. It was a far cry from Griffith's two-day productions, and presaged much that was to come in Hollywood.

In complete contrast, in 1930 Lang shot a modest-budget picture in a makeshift studio outside Berlin in six weeks – and this, above all else that is linked to his name, is the Fritz Lang film that illumines the history of the cinema, that was a landmark in the story of suspense on the screen, and that, after more than 40 years, can still draw the true film fan miles across country to catch a showing at some local film society.

It was Lang's first sound film. It was his own favourite of all his works. He was originally going to call it *The Murderers Among Us* (a title which

Madness, melodrama and murder in Fritz Lang's German period;
OPPOSITE (above & below) Dr. Mabuse der Spieler (*Atlas 1922*) *and* (bottom) *a movie simply titled* M (*Lang-Nero Film 1931*)
ABOVE & BELOW *The mammoth* Metropolis (*U.F.A. 1926*)

The pathetic and hunted child-killer Peter Lorre in M (Lang-Nero Film 1931)
OVERLEAF *Blackmail (British Int. Pictures 1929) — and Alfred Hitchcock directs Anny Ondra, the German actress who was the first of the blonde and beautiful "Hitchcock Heroines"*

annoyed the Nazis, who at first thought, wrongly, it was going to be a film about them), and it came out into the world with the one-letter title *M*.

It was a shocking idea for its time: a crime drama, not about a safely-larger-than-life mastermind, not about a dashing handsome hero with glamorous helpmate. It was a film about a plump little man with bulging eyes who was a pathological child-killer.

The idea was sparked by newspaper reports about a child-murderer named Peter Kürten, headlined as the Vampire of Düsseldorf. Lang set out by studying several murderers, he spent a week in a mental home to observe the inmates, and he even used real criminals in certain scenes in the film.

M embodies several Fritz Lang themes: the duality between justice and revenge, mob hysteria, the menacing anticipation of watching a helplessly trapped individual trying fruitlessly to escape as greater forces move inexorably in. And, for probably the first time in the cinema, it adds a new dimension to suspense: pity. For the killer is clearly mentally sick; he cannot overcome the overwhelming compulsion of his murderous disease; and yet, in almost documentary style, we see him hunted down and almost lynched as a criminal, rather than treated as a sick man.

The murderer was played by Peter Lorre (filming by day while acting on the stage by night), in a haunting performance that has scarcely been matched in all the scores of Hollywood thrillers he has made since.

The plot shows Lorre as the archetypal outsider – outside the law and society because of his compulsive crimes; outside the balancing society of the underworld because he is not a professional criminal, for gain, in their terms. Because the police hunt for him causes the law to lean too heavily on the beggars, thieves and counterfeiters of the city, the underworld organises to track him down. Lang intercuts from police conference to underworld meeting – and the latter, with its own mini-mastermind, is a sight more efficient. The criminal mob become an organisation of frightening order, networking the city with their own spies, and they it is who catch the murderer first. Then, when they stage their own "trial" of the killer – no longer a frightening menace: now a pathetic shred of warped humanity, trapped as much by his own disease as by any external force – they revert to hysterical mob violence and are on the point of lynching him when the police arrive to take him off for the trial of law.

It is perhaps a commentary on our times that in the most famous of all films about a pathological killer – Alfred Hitchcock's *Psycho* (1960) – Anthony Perkins lacked not only the menace of little Peter Lorre, but also the dimension of invoking our incredulous sympathy.

But then: Hitchcock has always insisted that *Psycho* was a fun film; and Lang unashamedly set out to make a social document.

Psycho, too, reeked with blood and horror, whereas the suspense of *M* was subtle. A child's balloon without an owner, a rolling ball, were enough to tell us that another murder had been committed. The audience, trapped in its seats, torn by ambivalent feelings towards the killer, watched him trapped as the net was pulled tight.

Early in the film, the killer was heard whistling the Grieg theme from "In the Hall of the Mountain King". This theme inexorably became imbued with menace; and when we saw no more than a girl looking in a shop window, the melody on the soundtrack told us chillingly that the murderer was there, just out of sight.

Of course, the operatic approach of adding a musical dimension to menace with a killer-theme on the soundtrack has been used many times since. The one savoured most pleasurably by the taste-buds of my memory was in Orson Welles's glorious mishmash of a suspense film, *Journey Into Fear* (1943), where the little killer obsessively played a scratchy old 78 rpm disc of someone singing "Chagrin d'Amour". The assassin was short and fat; his belly large, his jowls flabby. I do not recall his having a line of dialogue to speak. But the whole film was pervaded with heightened menace when he sat, his little round eyes blank behind his little round pebble lenses, listening compulsively to the atrociously scratchy record, jumbling the words of the song at the wrong speed, the needle jumping from groove to groove; his nerve-ends, unlike ours, immune to the discordancy.

Of such strokes is suspense made.

PLEASE KEEP AWAY
FROM Front
of CAMERA

THE START of a film: the head of a girl in close-up. She is very blonde, and her fair curls fill the screen. She is screaming. Cut to a theatre sign, announcing a show called "Tonight, Golden Curls". The lights of the sign are reflected in water. From that water the golden-curled girl is pulled to land. She is no longer screaming. She is dead. Murdered.

That scene was more than the start of a film. It was the start of what came to be known as "the Hitchcock touch" and, because of that, it was also the real start of suspense films in Britain.

The year was 1926 and the film was *The Lodger*.

There had been British suspense films before that. Alfred Hitchcock had directed films before that. But from the first moment of *The Lodger* (made four or five years before Lang's *M*) there was apparent an imaginative authority in the creation of thrillers that was to burgeon into the greatest professionalism the *genre* has known throughout Hitchcock's career. It is a pity that it did not burgeon so lavishly throughout the whole British film industry until many years later.

The Lodger, based on a novel by Mrs Belloc Lowndes, was set in a Jack the Ripper-type murder wave in a foggy London. The victims were always blonde girls, always murdered on the same day of the week. The killer wore a black cloak and carried a black bag.

While the whole capital speculates in panic, a new lodger turns up at a quiet boarding house. He wears a black cloak and carries a black bag. There are other details which cause the finger of suspicion to tremble towards him . . . so is he or isn't he the mass-murderer? Well, of course he isn't, because he's played by Ivor Novello, the patrician-profiled leading romantic actor of the day, and nobody would let him end up as a murderer; and so there developed, incidentally, from the demands of the box-office, a theme that was to dominate many of Hitchcock's later films: the innocent man wrongly accused.

(The problem of not being allowed to make a charming romantic star a killer faced Hitchcock again when he made *Suspicion* in Hollywood in 1941. Cary Grant was permitted to be a liar and a cad, albeit a loveable one: but if we had reflected on the then current rules of the business in regard to happy endings and not damaging star-images, we would have missed an awful lot of delicious tension in sitting through the whole movie wondering if Mr Grant really was trying to poison Joan Fontaine.)

One of the more memorable images in *The Lodger* was contrived when Hitchcock wanted to show the mysterious new guest pacing the floor of his upstairs room in agitation, over the heads of the family sitting below. Today we would probably hear his ominous footfalls, plodding in creepy cliché. But those were the days of silent cinema: no sound. So Hitchcock made a plate-glass floor for the lodger's room and photographed up from below, up past the hanging gas chandelier, through the shadowed glass, up to a new tension from a new perspective as those restless legs walked to and fro, to and fro.

There was a hint of the Hitchcock technique of surprise, of spurning the theatrical banality that was the curse of so many early British films, even before *The Lodger*. In 1925, the first film he ever directed to completion was a melodrama called *The Pleasure Garden*. At the climax, the villain goes off his head and is about to chop down the heroine with some cold steel when a doctor arrives and shoots him. Any other director at that time would have had the villain clutch his breast, totter across the screen with one arm outstretched to clutch the air, and his best profile towards the camera, to recline and make an Irving-like declaration of his sins before expiring. Not so the young Hitchcock. He had the shock of the bullet return the madman to his senses for an instant. He turned and said casually: "Oh, hello doctor." Then he noticed his own blood. "Oh," he said again – and collapsed and died.

The story of British suspense films of the late Twenties and the Thirties is really the story of the young Alfred Hitchcock, and his films include some of the few made in London in that decade which stand the test of time and could be seen again by later generations without risibility or stagey embarrassment.

In 1929, in a film called *Blackmail*, connoisseurs can observe the genesis of a long line of cool, elegant, frequently fair and always beautiful and discreetly sexual "Hitchcock heroines" with the casting of the German actress Anny Ondra. There is a hallmark, long and lovely and sterling and shining like silver, to these actresses. Recollect some of the names over the years: Madeleine Carroll, Grace Kelly, Tippi Hedren, Eva-Marie Saint, Ingrid Bergman, not to mention Kim Novak, Doris Day and Julie Andrews.

Back in the 1929 *Blackmail*, in Hitchcock's first talkie, the girl grabbed a knife and killed a man who tried to rape her. There is a remarkable scene at the family breakfast table the next morning. Cosy domestic chatter wafts over the girl's unlistening head, until only one word, repeated, reaches her

LEFT *Ivor Novello in Hitchcock's* The Lodger *(Gainsborough 1936) – symbolizing the agony of the innocent victim*
ABOVE & BELOW *A knife-edge coincidence linked the night before and the morning after in Hitchcock's* Blackmail *(British Int. Pictures 1929)*

ABOVE *Rehearsal for assassination. Peter Lorre, Leslie Banks and friends in
1934 version of* The Man Who Knew Too Much *(Gaumont British 1934)*
BELOW *The hero becomes American in the person of James Stewart in the
1955 remake of* The Man Who Knew Too Much *(Paramount-Filwite 1955)*

consciousness: "Knife, knife". And then she is politely asked to pass the bread knife: it looks like the one she had used for the killing.

This film was climaxed with one of Hitchcock's marvellous settings for a chase: the blackmailing villain was pursued through the British Museum, to fall to his death from the dome of the Reading Room.

Five years later, Hitchcock put together another bravura climactic of suspense with an idea that was so good that he was to use it twice. The film was *The Man Who Knew Too Much*, made first in England in 1934 with Leslie Banks, Edna Best, Frank Vosper, Nova Pilbeam, Pierre Fresnay and – fresh from *M* to make his first British film – Peter Lorre. In 1955 in Hollywood, Hitchcock remade the story with James Stewart and Doris Day (the latter relieving the tension by breaking into a chorus of "Whatever Will Be, Will Be" at appropriate moments).

In the English version the story opened in Switzerland; in the American, in Marrakesh. The basic story-line is about a couple of tourists who happen to witness the murder of a Frenchman who, with his dying words, tells them of a plot to assassinate an ambassador in London. And where is the assassination to take place? In the Albert Hall, during a concert, at the moment when the clash of cymbals will drown the sound of the shot.

ABOVE *Robert Donat (left), as the man on the run, takes shelter in a Scottish croft in* The Thirty-Nine Steps *(Gaumont British 1935)*
BELOW *Alfred Hitchcock directs the opening scenes in Marrakesh of* The Man Who Knew Too Much *(Paramount-Filwite 1955)*

Hitchcock creates superb tension as the villains rehearse, studying discs of the music to become familiar with the exact moment when the cymbals will clang. There is a long, stomach-wrenching sequence, quite without dialogue, in the concert hall as the music builds to the moment of murder while the wife, in the early version, the couple in the later one, desperately try to reach the ambassador to warn him. They fail – but the woman screams as the cymbals are about to meet and the shock puts the gunman off his aim.

But it was with *The Thirty-Nine Steps*, made in London in 1935, that Hitchcock showed the breathlessly fast-moving narrative, the swift-paced change of locale, the rapid succession of thrilling set-pieces that were to reach their fulfilment in the later Hollywood "chase" films such as *North by Northwest*.

And Hitchcock leavened the excitement with moments of romantic or sexual charm in scenes between Robert Donat and Madeleine Carroll which were the precursors of all those delectable scenes that were to come in later years between Cary Grant and Ingrid Bergman. How deliciously shocked were the audiences of 1935 when Mr Donat – who was on the run across the Scottish moors and had somehow got himself handcuffed to Miss Carroll – offered to help her off with her stockings!

Alfred Hitchcock in action . . .
directing The Secret Agent
(Gaumont British 1936)

This was a film which freed itself from the over-pedestrian constraints of plot. It never took off into fantasy: every incident was plausible in itself and in its context; and the headlong rush from excitement to excitement went at such a pace that there was never a moment in which to ask the dull old question: "Why?"

And what excitements they were – right from the early scene when Robert Donat, in bed, saw his door open and a mysterious woman clutching a piece of paper moved across the room towards him, then fell forward across his legs . . . and we realised with a chill that there was a knife in her back. From then on Robert Donat was on the run both from the police and the spy-ring (a situation echoed in Hitchcock's *Saboteur* in 1942, when Robert Cummings, also handcuffed for much of the time, was on the run from both sides of the law).

Such a library of memories is packaged in *The Thirty-Nine Steps* . . . Robert Donat escaping through a police station window, ducking into a hall where there is an election meeting, getting mistaken for a guest speaker and having to make a speech . . . escaping from a train on the Forth

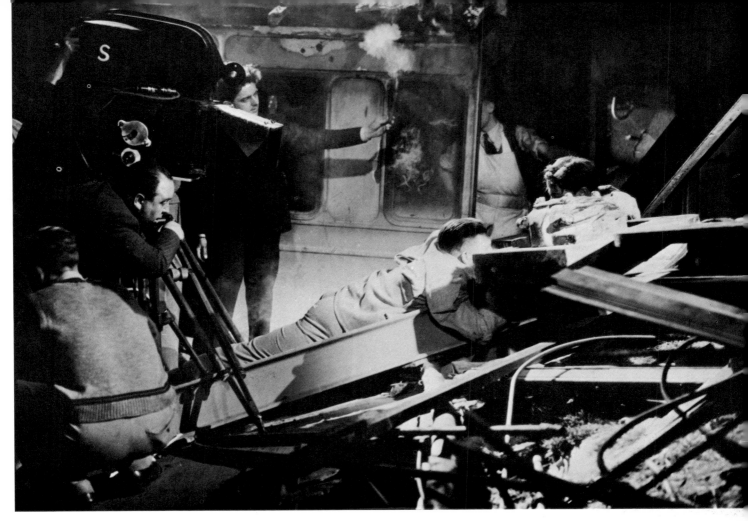

Bridge . . . suddenly recognising the master-villain when he notices a tell-tale finger missing from the right hand of his gentlemanly host . . . being shot and surviving when a bullet hits the Bible the previous owner had left in the pocket of his borrowed coat . . . escaping with Madeleine Carroll and the aid of a flock of sheep . . . and signing the death warrant of "Mr Memory", the music hall performer with infallible answers to all questions who was used to transmit messages by the spies, by asking him what is the secret of the thirty-nine steps, and hearing the man compulsively blurt out the truth.

To this day I cannot disentangle what the secret was; but, so potent were the excitements on the way to it, that it doesn't matter a damn.

Looking back on the train escape sequences of *The Thirty-Nine Steps*, one is reminded of how often trains have played a significant part in Hitchcock thrillers. *The Secret Agent* (1936), starring Madeleine Carroll, John Gielgud, Peter Lorre and Robert Young, was climaxed by a murderous train wreck. *The Lady Vanishes* (1938), starring Margaret Lockwood, Michael Redgrave, Dame May Whitty, and Basil Radford and Naunton

Wayne as the two cliché-Englishmen, virtually all took place on a trans-European express. *Saboteur* (1942), starring Robert Cummings and Priscilla Lane, was by no means one of the most powerful thrillers, but was memorable for the scene where the couple boarded a train and ended up in the circus freaks' carriage where, in theatrical moments that would have delighted the heart of an Orson Welles, the door was opened by a midget, the bearded lady had her whiskers done up in curlers and the Siamese twins were incorrigibly quarrelling. And, of course, there were the classic *Strangers on a Train* (1951), starring Robert Walker and Farley Granger, and the train scenes, sometimes symbolic and wittily sexy, in *North by Northwest* (1959), Cary Grant, Eva-Marie Saint, James Mason.

Some worthy student will no doubt one day construct a cinematic thesis out of the symbolic significance of trains in Hitchcock's work. The rest of us will just enjoy the effects he extracts from the power, the confined action, the compressed force . . . and recall with interest that, as a young man not yet in films, Hitchcock's hobby was train timetables, which he would make a point of learning off by heart.

The Day
of the
Private Eye

PRECEDING PAGES *Richard
Attenborough as the teenage gang
leader in* Brighton Rock *(Assoc.
British 1947)*
Humphrey Bogart, off and on screen
(above & below) *in John Huston's*
The Maltese Falcon *(Warners 1941)*
RIGHT *A generation on in time (but
not necessarily in technique), Goldie
Hawn counts the loot in* The Heist
(Frankovich 1971)
OVERLEAF *Meticulous planning and the
failure of a robbery was the key to the
suspense of* The Anderson Tapes
(Weitman 1971)

THERE WAS a golden time, an olden time, when me
really lived in suspense, and sudden death ar
tension and threat walked the world. And in th
time there flowered on the screen sudden death ar
tension and threat of a different order, which ha
nothing to do with the war and yet which someho
mirrored the pattern of the age.

Those years of the Forties, when Hollywoo
decided that the mystery thriller deserved big
budget, big-star treatment, threw up a new kind o
hero who was exactly right for his time: they wen
the years which established the private eye adven
ture as the irremovable all-time favourite in th
whole field of suspense.

The private eye was a loner. He had contact
and knew where to go for what he wanted, but h
had no apparent friends. He had very little money
and that was earned the hard way – and he wa
totally incorruptible. He had no fear, not jus
because he had seen it all before and there was n
trick a hood could pull that would surprise him
but because right and justice and solving his cas
were all that interested him, and he was wrapped i
the invisible armour of the tough good guy whe
he prowled the streets of the city in its dark place
of corruption and violence. He was laconic, but h
could throw a wisecrack as fast as he could throw
punch. He seemed to have only one suit, and h
had never got around to getting married, though h
had a sharp eye for a dame; but when they saic
Goodnight the chances were that he would go
back and hang his hat in his little glass-doorec
office, where there was a bottle of Scotch in the
filing cabinet for lonely consolation.

He was quintessentially Humphrey Bogart, o
course, but he was others too.

The man and the mood and the approach, anc
even the plots that were usually unimportantly
incomprehensible, were all there on paper, waiting
for Hollywood, in the mystery novels of Dashiel
Hammett and Raymond Chandler.

The field is so rich, the choice so lavish in that
decade, that it is difficult to know where memory
should stop and call "Encore". Perhaps with *The
Maltese Falcon* (1941), based on Dashiell Hammett's
novel. It was scripted by John Huston and was his
first film as a director. It was also the film début of
the menacingly mountainous Sidney Greenstreet,
who seemed to get more dangerous as he got more
imperturbably polite.

What a gallery of characters there was enmeshed
in the baffling – but never mind – coils of plot
centreing on the hunt for possession of a priceless
antiquity, the statuette of the Maltese falcon itself.

Humphrey Bogart was Sam Spade, of the private detective firm of Spade and Archer, and it soon became a one-man firm when Mr Archer stopped living early in the movie. People had a habit of abruptly and permanently giving up breathing when they crossed the path of Mary Astor, who started out as Sam Spade's client, but who we learned in the end was as deadly as she was beautiful. There was a wonderful closing scene when we wondered if Bogart would yield to the blandishments and entreaties of Mary Astor and save her from prison and, possibly, the gas chamber. But we did not wonder for long: he was incorruptible to the bitter end – and bitter it was – and he watched them take her away.

And who could forget the minor cameos of villainy? Peter Lorre, pin-striped and gardenia-d, primped and, one imagined, perfumed, as the sibilant Joel Cairo; Elisha Cook Jr, bulging-eyed and perpetually piqued, as Sidney Greenstreet's gunman, because he was not allowed to finish off Bogart.

I could see that film a dozen times – and as a matter of fact, I have.

There were many attempts to recreate on the screen Raymond Chandler's immortal character, Philip Marlowe, and probably the first serious effort was in 1944, with Edward Dmytryk directing. The film was called *Farewell My Lovely* in Britain and *Murder, My Sweet* in the United States. The plot, as always with this genre, mattered far less than the characters and the action: it was sparked when Marlowe was hired to find an ex-convict's girl friend. This Marlowe was played by Dick Powell. He made a bold, successful effort to drop his all-singing, all-dancing image, and he was tough enough; but he was a little too charming, a shade too superficial, to suggest the depths and the strengths of the real Marlowe.

Humphrey Bogart was the man to do this above all others. And he did it superbly in Howard Hawks's *The Big Sleep* in 1946. This stuck closely to Raymond Chandler's novel except for the end, which was changed to avoid making Lauren Bacall a murderess. Elisha Cook Jr was there again; and Dorothy Malone as the girl working in a bookshop which fronts a porn trade.

Don't try to recall the details of the plot. Chandler himself once said: "The mystery and the solution are only the olive in the Martini, and the really good mystery is one you would read even if you knew somebody had torn out the last chapter." The same went for the movie. There were at least half-a-dozen murders in it, and Howard Hawks said

after making it that he still did not know who had committed one of them.

The moments were all: the chemistry between Bogart and Bacall, the fast-moving action, the toughness that was an escapism and not a brutality. When it first appeared, *The Big Sleep* was attacked in some quarters for violence and amorality – but beneath its cynicism and toughness there breathed a heart and sentimentality which help to make it timeless.

Private eyes, assorted vintages;
LEFT *Burt Reynolds in action in*
Shamus *(Columbia/Weitman 1972)*
ABOVE *Dick Powell in* Farewell My
Lovely *(R.K.O. 1944)*
BELOW *Humphrey Bogart and
Lauren Bacall in* The Big Sleep
(WB 1946)

ABOVE & BELOW *Robert Montgomery,
playing Philip Marlowe in* Lady in the
Lake *(MGM 1946), was only seen when
he looked in a mirror*
RIGHT *Edward G. Robinson was the
investigator, Fred MacMurray and
Barbara Stanwyck the passionate
conspirators in* Double Indemnity
(Paramount 1944)

A big problem to some Marlowe fanatics when their hero was transferred to the screen was that his subjectivity was lost. In Raymond Chandler's novels, Marlowe told his stories in the first person: the reader went only where Marlowe went, met whom he met, knew only what he knew. The all-seeing, third-personal eye of the camera brought a detachment, a distancing from Marlowe – or so some thought. One of these was Robert Montgomery, the actor who turned director in 1946 to make *The Lady in the Lake*, using the camera as Marlowe. We, the audience, saw through Marlowe's eyes – which meant, for example, that we never saw Robert Montgomery, playing the lead, unless he looked in a mirror. It also meant some shock moments when a character punched Marlowe, who was the camera, who was *us*, in the face; and when another character shoved his face at us through a car window and *our* fist whammed up to hit him.

A lot of fuss was made about the technique at the time, and there was much high-falutin' talk about the innovation of the subjective camera. In fact it did not add to the suspense, and was far from revolutionary. As Raymond Chandler commented: "The camera-eye technique is old stuff in Hollywood. Every young writer or director has wanted to try it."

Of course, there were some superb thrillers coming out of Hollywood in that decade which did not depend on the private eye conventions – but somehow the best of them were pervaded by the same cynicism, the same realism, the same ruthless suspense. Best of all, to my taste for thrills, was Billy Wilder's *Double Indemnity*, made in 1944. It was adapted from the novel by James M. Cain and was based on a real-life murder in New York in 1927, when a wife and her lover killed the husband for his insurance money. In the film, a near-breaking-point tension was reached and sustained in the passion of Fred MacMurray and Barbara Stanwyck – a passion for each other and for money; in the murder of her husband; and in their unavailing attempts to escape the investigating shrewdness of Edward G. Robinson. The suspense was cathartically harrowing: one could not have endured more – so perhaps the producers were wise in their decision to cut from the release print scenes of Fred MacMurray's execution.

This was the film which took Raymond Chandler to Hollywood to work on the script with the brilliant, demanding Billy Wilder. Afterwards, Chandler wryly described it as an agonizing experience which had doubtless shortened his life –

ABOVE & BELOW *The execution scenes from* Double Indemnity *(Paramount 1944) which were cut because they were thought to be too harrowing*
OPPOSITE *Richard Attenborough, razor, and near-victim in* Brighton Rock *(Assoc. British 1947)*

but had taught him as much about screenwriting as he was ever likely to know.

And anything which could teach Chandler about mystery writing was a film for the record books.

When I look back on the dates at which such films were made, it is hard now to believe that they were around *before* the thriller which was hailed by so many people as a post-war peak of British suspense films. *Brighton Rock* (re-titled *Young Scarface* in USA) was made in 1947 by the Boulting Brothers from a screenplay by Graham Greene and Terence Rattigan based on Greene's powerful novel about home-grown gangsters led by a vicious 17-year-old, Pinkie Brown (Richard Attenborough).

The story was strong enough. The setting, Brighton, with its pier and pubs and fortune tellers and racetrack, could lend itself to some highly-coloured set-pieces. But oh dear dear and tut tut: those gangsters! Artificial, cosy, actorish, they were a million light years from the reality of the British underworld. When everything had to depend on the menace engendered by the pathological teenager and his thugs, one wondered, not only why their newspaperman quarry did not go to the police, but why he didn't simply turn and say "Boo!" When Pinkie drew a razor, I felt not so much like recoiling in horror from a cold-blooded slashing, as inquiring gently: "Are you sure you're old enough to shave, sonny?"

It is incredible to me that *Brighton Rock*, for all its distinguished names, came from the same decade as *Double Indemnity* or *The Big Sleep*. I can only assume that all those who praised it so lavishly were flushed with a post-war national pride. Alas, for the critic, patriotism should not be enough.

Trapped!

THERE IS no more powerful way to turn the screws of suspense than to compress and confine your characters in space and in time. The lesson was learned to classic effect in the first of all the many *Phantom of the Opera* films, produced by Carl Laemmle and directed by Rupert Julian, in 1925. Lon Chaney was the first of the long line of Phantoms and the one against whom all his successors had to be measured.

The story, despite all its variants, is the familiar one of the musician shunning the world because of his disfigurement and retreating to a hideout beneath the Opera House, whence he emerges to terrorise singers and audience alike. He kidnaps a young girl singer – perhaps to teach her to become a great star; certainly because, in his grotesque and pathetic way, he loves her – and carries her off to a boudoir he has prepared far underground.

There was melodrama galore: in the first version, for example, two would-be rescuers found themselves trapped in an un-cosy mirrored room the Phantom had prepared, where they first got a heat treatment and then were flooded. But, beyond all the heightened effects, it was the pathos of the Phantom underscoring his lonely menace which gave the character a dimension, and the isolation of the captor and his captive, confined to a literal underworld, which gave the suspense of the whole film its power.

It was all as far from real life as anyone could conceive it and, in 1925, none the worse for that. But if, instead of larger-than-life grotesques, the characters are quiet, happy, ordinary people, living an untroubled and natural domestic life, and *then* they are trapped with deadly menace . . . then you have suspense-plus.

This was the realisation of writer Joseph Hayes with a novel, a play based upon it, and then a film script written for producer-director William Wyler in 1955. Its title: *The Desperate Hours*, and a towering achievement in suspense films it was.

It was cast to perfection; written and directed with immaculate authority. Its basic situation – of a family trapped in their home for 36 hours by an utterly ruthless gang – was not new. What was new and immeasurably compelling was the fact that these were not simply "good guys" and "bad guys", but all were real, breathing, vulnerable human beings: they all knew how to hate and to be afraid, and to want to kill and want to love. There were no supermen: they got hungry, and irritable, and tired, and they showed hesitation and uncertainty as well as pure courage.

It began as an ordinary day for the Hilliard

family in their pleasant home in Indianapolis. Eleanor gave breakfast to her family and saw them off – husband Dan to his job in a store, pretty daughter Cindy to her office desk, and ten-year-old Ralphie to school. Turning on the radio, she paid little attention to the news item about the escape of three desperate criminals from jail: ruthless Glenn Griffin, his younger brother Hal and the brutish Kobish. These three needed a safe hideout while they awaited the arrival of some expected money – and they chose the Hilliard home. They were installed and completely in command when Dan and the two youngsters came home – and there the family was trapped, under the gangsters' order to "make it normal" and with no doubt of the consequences if they did not obey.

As the major tensions mounted – the money did not arrive and the police closed in – there was a fascinating interplay of lesser conflicts. The father (Fredric March) urgently trying to repress his rage to save his family – until his final gamble. The schoolboy (Richard Eyer) unable to believe that the guns and bullets are real – and unable to understand why his adored father is apparently submitting without a fight. The wife (Martha Scott) fighting hysteria in an attempt to live unsuspiciously normally in such circumstances. The spitfire daughter

PRECEDING PAGES *Suspense in a studio tank : Tallulah Bankhead and John Hodiak (together right) with fellow survivors in* Lifeboat *(20th Century-Fox 1943)*
ABOVE LEFT *The cosy domestic setting for terror in* The Desperate Hours *(Paramount 1955)*
ABOVE *Mrs Eleanor Roosevelt and (right) William Wyler visit Humphrey Bogart and Fredric March on set*
BELOW *Bogart, scarred by the make-up department, talks with producer Bill Perlberg*

At both ends of the gun . . . (above) *Humphrey Bogart threatened by Edward G. Robinson in* Key Largo *(Warners 1936) . . .* (above right) *Bogart threatening Bette Davis and Leslie Howard in* The Petrified Forest *(Warners 1936)*
BELOW RIGHT *Drinka-Pinta-Feara-Day. Terence Stamp in* The Collector *(The Collector Co. 1965)*

(Mary Murphy) and her boy-friend (Gig Young), whose impatient courtship almost causes disaster. The youngest criminal (Dewey Martin) coming to see in the quiet normality of the lives he has invaded a message of the waste of his own. Even the police – Arthur Kennedy leading the hunt and knowing he has been marked out for murder; his men, unsure whether you stay away from the house in the hope of saving the hostages, or whether you bring up the machine-guns and risk slaughtering the innocent in order to eliminate the guilty. And, above all, the gang leader, played by Humphrey Bogart with an intelligence to match his deadly ruthlessness, with a shrewd instinct for discovering others' weaknesses; torn when his own younger brother quits; finding himself as much a prisoner in the house as his hostages.

It was in *The Petrified Forest*, back in 1936, that as Duke Mantee Bogart established himself as the definitive screen gangster. Now, in *The Desperate Hours*, he surpassed even that performance.

It is difficult to resist the temptation to compare *The Desperate Hours* with *Key Largo*, directed in 1948 by John Huston.

Here again the drama arose when a gangster and his thugs sought a temporary hideout by moving in on an innocent family, and were unable to get away until a raging hurricane had blown itself out. The family were Lionel Barrymore, complete with wheelchair, and Lauren Bacall, wasp-waisted and – apparently without make-up – stunningly attractive. Their home was a small hotel in Florida, and "just passing through" was a tough and somewhat mixed-up good guy: Humphrey Bogart. The gangster was Edward G. Robinson.

With such a cast it could not fail to hold the attention. Yet, for all its workmanlike craft, it did not reach the level of Wyler's *The Desperate Hours*. Bogart, as *Key Largo*'s disillusioned war veteran who could not rouse himself to action until the last few minutes, left one frustrated: looking for the vicious power that he was to show as the gangster

in the later film. Edward G. Robinson, command-
ing, convincing, was still not so coldly *frightening* a
villain as Humphrey Bogart. And . . . an educational
speculation for scriptwriters: one can imagine how
the idea of the storming hurricane appealed at the
time. The violence and the drama outside, as the
wind tore at the palm trees and the waves threatened
to swallow the little wooden hotel, would surely
underscore and heighten the tensions within. . . .

Not so; and not only because the studio storm
was not always up to Nature's level. What Joseph
Hayes and William Wyler realised was that the
suspense of innocence trapped as hostages by
wickedness was vastly heightened by the contrast
with a quiet, undramatic, everyday setting. No
hurricane was needed to put the desperation in
The Desperate Hours.

In 1965 William Wyler once again tested the
limits of suspense by confining them when he
directed *The Collector*, based on John Fowles'
remarkable novel, for the lively young American
producers John Kohn and Jud Kinberg, who were
then operating from London. The story was rather
different. Freddie Clegg (Terence Stamp) was an
insignificant, ill-adjusted London bank clerk with
the hobby of collecting and mounting butterflies.

ABOVE *The body is in the chest . . . James Stewart and murderers in* Rope
(Transatlantic Pictures 1948)
RIGHT *The body is in the garden . . . Grace Kelly and suspect neighbour in*
Rear Window *(Patron Inc./Hitchcock 1954)*

From a safe distance, he was fascinated by the young art student Miranda Grey (Samantha Eggar). Then, when he won the football pools, he decided to add Miranda to his collection. He bought a house with a strong cellar in a quiet district. He furnished the cellar in his own atrocious idea of good taste: a record player, lots of classical discs, art books, plenty of clothes in Miranda's size. And then he kidnapped Miranda and carted her off to his cellar.

The suspense here – and suspense there was in awaiting the unguessable outcome – was in the interplay of the two characters shut up in those four walls for two long months. The distraught and unbelieving Miranda tried every woman's wile, every appeal to reason; while the insecure Clegg, subtly her social inferior, determined to keep her there until she came to love him. Shades here of *Phantom of the Opera*, oddly enough, when misfit Lon Chaney told his victim: "I have brought you five cellars deep . . . because I love you."

Naturally, the old maestro of suspense, Alfred Hitchcock, could not resist the temptations of confined time and space in which to spin his spells. One of his more interesting attempts was in his first colour film, *Rope*, made in 1948. Hitchcock directed a script by Arthur Laurents from Patrick Hamilton's play. The story was about two upper-crust young Americans, John Dall and Farley Granger, who strangled a college friend just for kicks and hid his body in a chest in the room to which his parents were coming to a cocktail party. Among the guests was James Stewart, who sifted out the truth before the evening was over.

One could imagine what Hitchcock would do with such a situation – but in fact he did a great deal more. For a start, he played out the drama *in the actual time* of the story: 81 minutes on a summer evening in that New York flat. He dispensed with the usual cutting techniques and, for the first time in history, shot in ten-minute takes, with not a single interruption for the different camera set-ups. The walls and furniture moved on silent rollers out of shot to let the camera pass. He had a semi-circular background of the New York skyline made up with moveable clouds of spun glass; and he drew up a special working plan to move the clouds gradually between the ten-minute reels so that the sky would always tell the truth as time passed. Even this perfectionism was not enough: by sunset, Hitchcock realised that the orange in the sun was too strong – so he shot the last five reels again.

You cannot confine your character much more than to break his leg, stick it in a cast, and keep him in a wheelchair in one room of his apartment from beginning to end of a murder mystery – and that is precisely what Hitchcock did to James Stewart in the unforgettable *Rear Window* (1954).

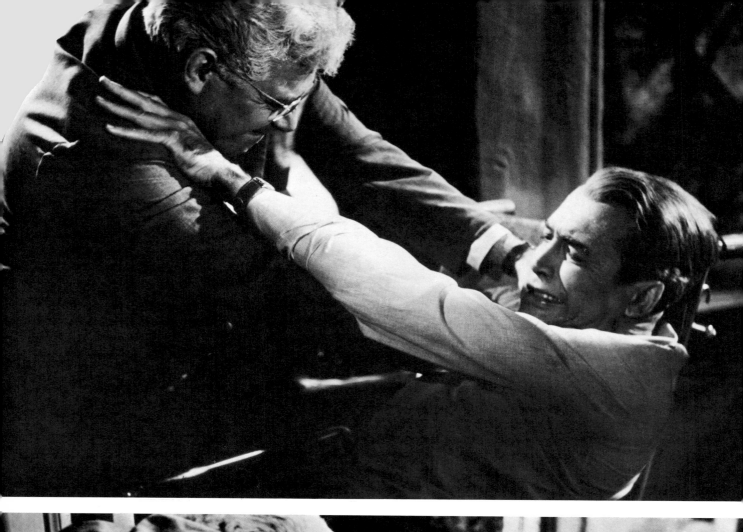

This was not only a film of great suspense and some humour: it also appealed strongly to the *voyeur* in all of us because the script (by John Michael Hayes from a story by Cornell Woolrich) gave the confined and crippled James Stewart little else to do but gaze through his window into the apartments across the courtyard. Apart from one scene, the camera never left his room; and from it, with his eyes, we saw a little universe of human nature in microcosm.

Within a period of three days and nights (the time as confined as the space), Stewart comes to suspect that one of these neighbours has murdered his wife and hidden her body in a flower bed in the courtyard below. Now the helpless Stewart has to prove his suspicions to the girl-friend he can't quite bring himself to marry (ah, the ice-cool Grace Kelly in trim jeans), to his detective friend (Wendell Corey) and to his disbelieving nurse (Thelma Ritter).

All the while, the people in the 31 apartments that he can see live out their little lives. There is a musician who, at the beginning, is toying with a few bars and, by the end, has completed his composition – but not without temperamental setbacks, fits of despair and some roistering parties. There is the lonely woman, laying table for dinner for a lover who will never come because he does not exist. There are the newlyweds, making love all the time; the young dancer perpetually practising; and the childless couple who sleep on the fire escape and every morning lower their little baby-substitute dog from their fifth storey apartment down to the courtyard. When the dog is found dead, having spent too much time sniffing around the fateful courtyard, Stewart has another support for his suspicions: all the neighbours rush to their windows to stare down into the yard except the suspected murderer. He sits quietly smoking in the dark.

Stewart, a photographer, has a telephoto lens to help his prying – and when he notices that the flowers in the yard are closer to the earth than they were when he first saw them, two days earlier, he has another clue.

Grace Kelly braves the suspect's rooms and finds the missing woman's wedding ring: would a wife "go away" and leave behind her wedding ring?

In the end, the killer realises that he is being watched, and tries to kill Stewart who, helpless in his wheelchair, can only try to defend himself with photographic flashbulbs. Stewart is saved at the last moment, of course, but he gets his other leg broken in the process – and it's back to the wheelchair.

LEFT *Out of the* Rear Window *(Patron Inc./Hitchcock 1954) goes James Stewart to end up back in the wheelchair* (below) *where it all began*

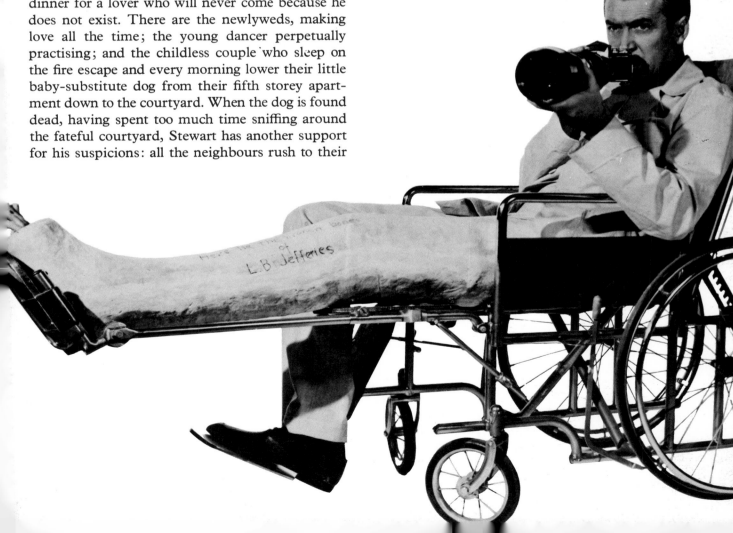

ABOVE *Barbara Stanwyck sees her killer approach in* Sorry, Wrong Number
(Hal Wallis 1948)
RIGHT *George Segal gets tough in* The Quiller Memorandum *(Rank/
Foxwell/Carthay 1966)*
OVERLEAF *Bare hands beat blue steel again in* Shamus *(Columbia/Weitman
1972)*

There was an earlier film which nags at my memory. It lacked the humour and humanity of *Rear Window*, it was more relentlessly frightening, and, like *Rear Window*, it exerted its grip because of the helplessness of the principal character, confined to one room. This was *Sorry, Wrong Number*, directed by Anatole Litvak in 1948 from a screenplay by Lucille Fletcher based on her own radio play.

Barbara Stanwyck played – with terrifying conviction – a wealthy, neurotic, partly paralysed, bedridden woman, alone at night in her New York home with only the telephone for company because her husband, Burt Lancaster, has given the staff the night off. Telephoning to see why her husband is not back from his office, Barbara Stanwyck gets a crossed line and hears two men discussing a murder which one of them has been paid to do that night: paid by a husband who wants to get rid of his rich, neurotic and bedridden wife whose

servants have been given the night off. At first, Barbara Stanwyck does not realise that she is to be the victim. Then, as the killing hour approaches, she does realise. In mounting panic she starts telephoning – the police, her doctor, anywhere for help (that bedside telephone has a star role to play). So hysterical is the poor neurotic woman that nobody believes her. Then, at the time mentioned by the killer on the phone, she hears someone coming up the stairs towards her room. The phone rings again. It is Burt Lancaster: he has changed his mind: he wants to call off the murder. But his terrified wife has dropped the phone, the killer's hands are already at her throat. She is murdered. The killer picks up the dangling phone. "Sorry, wrong number," he says into it, and puts back the receiver.

End of film. Total shattering of audience. And three harmless little words have suddenly become the most chilling in the language.

More than one director has realised that the perfect plausible way of confining your characters to germinate suspense is to put them in a boat – a mini-world of people, unable to get away from each other and isolated in the vast impersonal ocean with perils of its own. Hitchcock went one better (again). He stripped his people of almost all the amenities, even the necessities, of life, and put them in a lifeboat – and there they, and the camera, stayed for the whole film.

Lifeboat was made in 1943 with a script by Jo Swerling from a story by John Steinbeck. Since confined space and compressed action have a way of giving star moments to all the players, let's for once name the whole cast: Tallulah Bankhead, William Bendix, Walter Slezak, Mary Anderson, John Hodiak, Henry Hill, Heather Angel, Hume Cronyn, Canada Lee.

It was set at the time of its making – in World War II. An Allied ship was sunk by a German U-boat and a mixed bunch of survivors got away in the lifeboat. The enemy submarine was also sunk by the explosion and its Nazi commander (though believed then to be just an ordinary seaman) joined the survivors in their lifeboat. At first they were prepared to throw him overboard – but it was his skill which saved their little craft and gradually, while the allies were torn by dissension, selfishness, divided aims and views, his single-minded strength of purpose and his disciplined abilities took command. Unknown to the others, he was stealing their rations to keep up his strength, and steering them towards a rendezvous with a German supply ship. A wounded seaman discovered his secret: the Nazi threw him overboard in the night. He told the others it was suicide, but when they realised the truth they turned on him like a pack of wolves and killed the enemy who was also their saviour. There was a final climax: just as the German supply ship reached them, it too was sunk by an Allied vessel which turned up in time to save the lifeboat.

I see that François Truffaut, in his marathon interviews with Hitchcock (published in Britain by Secker and Warburg, and the best book on Hitchcock's work ever produced) commented that *Lifeboat* was "the very opposite of a thriller". I disagree. It *was* a thriller, but a flawed one for reasons which I attribute in part to the needs of wartime propaganda and in part to a frequent weakness of Hitchcock's in characterisation.

It was a thriller from the mounting tensions of the interplay of conflicting characters, trapped and isolated in the planks of their little boat. It was

LEFT *A battered Elizabeth Ashley screaming her head off in* The Third Day *(WB 1965)*
BELOW *William Bendix (right) learns he must lose a leg in* Lifeboat *(20th Century-Fox 1943)*

flawed because, in the effort to put across a message, Hitchcock permitted his characters to be stereotypes, symbols.

Raymond Chandler perceived this tendency in the director when he worked with Hitchcock on a script for *Strangers on a Train*. "His idea of characters is rather primitive," Chandler commented later. "Nice Young Man, Society Girl, Frightened Woman, Sneaky Old Beldame, Spy, Comic Relief, and so on."

In *Lifeboat* we had Communist Stoker, Fascist Businessman, Selfish Woman Journalist, Pretty Young Nurse, Nice Negro, and the rest: stock types.

Tallulah Bankhead, incidentally, dominated the acting of the whole fine cast except possibly Walter Slezak, as the Nazi. As the woman journalist, clinging to her material possessions, and only reluctantly thawing, she gave a performance with the power and the sting of a 30ft. salt wave.

It is ironic that the film's propaganda message, which I believe weakened and over-simplified it, was widely misunderstood at the time. Hitchcock intended to show at that stage of the war that the democracies should settle their differences and unite forces against the common enemy, who was disciplined, strong, and knew just where he was going. Instead, a lot of people attacked the film for

Hot pants and cold water in
The Poseidon Adventure
(Kent 1972)

showing the strongest character as the Nazi!

It is possible to go one better than a lifeboat for oceanic claustrophobia. What you do is have a luxury liner completely capsized by a monstrous wave spewed from a submarine earthquake, and you let ten people live on in a pocket of air, their only hope being to make their way through the flooded and corpse-strewn bowels of the sinking ship to a propeller shaft, where the hull is thinnest and where there is a chance of rescuers cutting their way through.

This was the terrific idea set up in a novel by Paul Gallico, which descended with awful disappointment on to the screen in 1973.

No one could ask for a better set-up for suspense – naturally, when the genesis was with that old master of mass emotions, Gallico. But oh, what a waste was there in *The Poseidon Adventure*.

Partly it was due to the lack of the technical perfectionism of a Hitchcock, who knows how to photograph a boat in a studio tank without making it look about as lifelike as a duck in a baby's bath. Much more was it due to the stereotyping of the characters and the excruciating banality of their dialogue. There was a nice muscular parson to lead, a nice Jewish couple still stickily in love after a couple of centuries of marriage, a nice tough detective and his nice reformed prostitute wife, a nice young girl (plus nice younger brother) and a nice girl singer who were there presumably to give a nice show of leg in hotpants and unladdered tights through thick and thin, a nice shy little draper and a nice cool steward.

Gene Hackman was cast as the preacher – the most unlikely reverend I could imagine. Presumably he was chosen because of his well-deserved success as the rough, tough detective in *The French Connection*. He played the parson every bit as rough and tough. Whenever he heaved his muscles and opened his mouth I expected a little balloon to come out, proclaiming: "I got the God connection."

But one must not blame the cast. There were fine actors among them and it was not their fault that the situations were patently prefabricated, that the characters were as realistic as the cutouts on the back of a cereal packet, living and dying as contrived "incidents".

A wonderful basic situation for aficionados of suspense. But for me at least, weaned on suspense movies, drugged by them and addicted to them, and with yardsticks by which to measure, the suspense leaked away through the worn old hull of the SS *Poseidon*.

Before leaving the sea and returning to shore, I want to recall briefly a film which, while not confined to it, was enacted largely on a yacht. This was a film imbued with a very different sort of suspense from that which was featured in our choices so far. There was no violence. The suspense was hinted at, suggested, refined tautly, glimpsed, did-he-mean-what-I-think-he-meant? It was implicit and subtle and mesmerising. It had artistic integrity and, lest that should frighten anyone away, it was commercially sufficiently on-target to bring its young director from Poland to a career in the West.

It was *Knife in the Water*, made in 1961 by Roman Polanski.

The story was simple enough. A rich, status-conscious, middle-aged man and his beautiful young wife gave a lift to a student and together they week-ended on the businessman's yacht. And there, in 48 hours in the sun, the tensions between this trio built, suspended, interwove as delicately and as clingingly as a spider's web.

The rich man's confidence was in his *possessions*, among which was numbered his wife, lying tanning, bikini-filling, tantalising, between them on the deck. The student's confidence, casual, almost unaware, was in his very *being*. The husband resented the youth, the strength, the "cool", the easy virility of the student and worked out a compulsion to keep challenging them, to try to show

his superiority. Polanski was fair – each had his own strengths and skills; but the one obsessively resented the other's. It was synthesised in a magnificent scene when the husband put out his hand, palm down, and the student stabbed a darting, playful, deadly knife between the spread fingers.

Ambiguous, equivocal, true of its time, the revealing of a generation gap before the phrase became glib – and of the stuff of which suspense is made.

No matter if we cannot pronounce the names; the cast deserve recording: Leon Niemczyk as the husband; Jolanta Umecka as the wife; Zygmunt Malanowicz as the student.

After he came to England, Polanski directed another strange kind of a suspense film in 1966: *Cul-de-Sac*. Here he isolated his characters in an old castle on Holy Island, off the Northumberland coast. And what characters they were: Donald Pleasance, putting on his wife's nightie and using her make-up in the retreat to which he had escaped from the unappealing world; Françoise Dorléac as the stunning bird; and Lionel Stander as the savage intruder blundering in.

A lot of critics gave a lot of praise to this film – presumably on the precept that if it's bizarre and a bit perverse and nobody understands it, it must be good. I regret that I found it just too bizarre, too perverse, too indulgently incomprehensible to sustain the suspense that must have been intended. I had a feeling that the freedom of the West had maybe gone to Mr Polanski's head.

LEFT *Director Roman Polanski first attracted attention in the West with his Polish film* Knife in the Water *(Film Polski, Kamera Unit 1961) and* RIGHT *He isolated Donald Pleasance and Françoise Dorleac on Holy Island in the British-made* Cul-de-Sac *(Compton Tekli 1966)* OVERLEAF *A small boy 'cried wolf' once too often in* The Window *(RKO 1948)*

The Helpless Ones

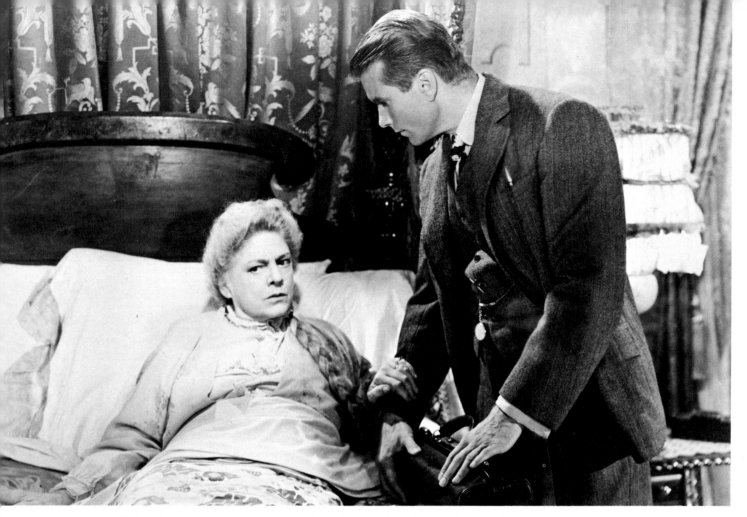

Ethel Barrymore was the bed-ridden mistress (above) *and Dorothy McGuire
the girl who could not speak* (below) *in* The Spiral Staircase *(RKO 1946)*
RIGHT *Bobby Driscoll was the boy nobody would believe in* The Window
(RKO 1948)

THE EXTRA vulnerability of the handicapped has
been a magnet to attract some fine practitioners of
suspense.

One such film that stands out in memory was
The Spiral Staircase, made in 1945 by the first-class
RKO team of Dore Schary producing, Robert
Siodmak directing, Mel Dinelli scripting (from a
novel by Ethel Lina White).

The fulcrum of the plot was the fact that the
beautiful and expressive Dorothy McGuire was
dumb – deprived of her speech by shock. Her terror
when death stalked had to be wordless, and it was
all the more potent. She could not communicate,
she could not plead or call for help.

It was New England in 1906, and she was
employed by the bedridden mistress (Ethel Barrymore) of an old house. On the girl's day off, a lame
girl was found murdered in the little town. It was
the third such murder. In each case the victim had
been physically handicapped – and, as we learned
later, the murderer killed because he could not
tolerate imperfection.

There was a chilling start to the suspense as Dorothy McGuire walked home through a night riven by storm, rattling a twig against railings. In a lightning flash we saw – but she did not – the silhouette of a man watching her. On into the house and, as she paused on a landing, we saw the feet of the man on another landing . . . waiting. And then, in a close-up of his eye, we saw her face reflected – an imperfect face; a face without a mouth.

On this level the tension was maintained in tautly visual terms, through the murder of another girl in the house and the mute's discovery of the body, and her belief that she knows the murderer. She tricks him into a room and locks him in . . . but, as she is to find, she has locked up the wrong man. At the very climax, when she seems helpless, without hope of escape, the shock restores her voice, she can scream for help – and the killer is shot.

One emerged from the cinema feeling as exhausted by terror as Miss McGuire had been.

The same writer, Mel Dinelli, with Dore Schary again in charge of production and Ted Tetzlaff, a former cameraman, directing, was responsible for another outstanding but much underrated thriller in that era, in which the victim was vulnerable simply because he was a child. This was *The Window*, which did not get the attention it deserved when it was made in 1948 because it ran only 73 minutes (and not a second of padding among them) and this was considered to be second-feature length.

The central figure was a ten-year-old boy (Bobby Driscoll), living in a New York tenement and known to everyone there as a teller of fantastic stories. His parents (Arthur Kennedy and Barbara Hale) warned him he must stop his fantasies . . . and what followed was a classic up-dating of the boy who cried "Wolf" once too often.

One stifling night, the boy climbed out on to a fire escape to seek cool air and, through a crack under a window blind, he witnessed a murder. He knew no one would believe him although this time, for the first time, his story was true. He tried to tell his mother that he had seen a couple called Kellerson trying to rob a drunk and killing him in a fight: the boy got scolded for his imagination and sent to bed. His father locked him in for punishment; the boy escaped and took his story to the police station. A detective investigated, but could find no body, no signs of a struggle.

Now the awful irony: the guilty Kellersons learn through the detective that the boy had seen them committing the crime, and the boy's parents, with terrifyingly understandable logic, send the boy to the killers to apologise "for spreading such an awful story about them".

The Kellersons cannot decide: should they leave well alone, as nobody believes the boy; or should they commit another crime to cover the first? They decide to murder him. He flees, but is chased and caught and taken to an abandoned, condemned, burned-out building. There he escapes and the killers pursue him perilously through

the crumbling building. Even when Kellerson falls to his death, the boy is not safe: a staircase collapses and leaves him stranded six floors up. But don't worry: he jumps into a safety net and ends up the pride of the neighbourhood.

To be blind, robbed of the power even to see the peril that threatens you, is a nightmare vulnerability. It also – naturally, plausibly, without obvious contrivance – gives the storyteller the opportunity effortlessly to fulfil one of the groundrules of suspense: let the audience know more than the main character. When we can see imminent danger which the victim, by definition, cannot see, the screw is tightened on the audience; we long to cry out in warning, but we cannot. We can only sit, deliciously helplessly, and wait to see what transpires. And when the victim is a young and beautiful woman, there is a poignant extra tug on the puppet-master's strings.

Two notable films in this genre would have been powerful suspense plots in any event, but in each case the personality (and the looks) of the leading actress contributed an additional assault on our emotions.

In *Blind Terror* (1971), written by Brian Clemens and directed by Richard Fleischer, the blind girl Sarah was portrayed by Mia Farrow. She had lost her sight in a fall from her horse, but had come to terms with her handicap and was serene, gay, happy to be reunited with her former lover, Steve

(Norman Eshley). Then the first threads of menace appear: a man, seen only as a pair of high-heeled cowboy-style boots, watches the family constantly. We become aware of his envy of their security and their money, and of Sarah's happiness at being home.

And then the menace crescendoes into stark horror. Returning home from a ride with Steve, Sarah discovers the bodies, one by one, of her family, murdered in her absence.

Can you imagine – or recall – the awful progression of such a discovery in a sightless world? Petrified in her darkness, Sarah stumbles towards the kitchen, to get out for help. She opens the wrong door and falls down the cellar steps. Recovering consciousness, she hears footsteps overhead.

She makes it to the hall, feels her way towards the front door – but it opens towards her and the family gardener is there, shot in the stomach, trying to warn her, collapsing.

Now gripped by panic, Sarah makes her way cautiously to the stables, gets her horse and gallops off – only to be thrown and left alone in the deserted countryside.

There is more to come. She staggers on, meets a gypsy, gasps out her story to him. Unsuspectingly, she hands over her one piece of vital evidence – a broken bracelet inscribed "Jacko". We can see, but she cannot, the man's look of alarm as he grabs it from her.

*Blindness adds a frightening
dimension to . . .
LEFT Mia Farrow in Blind Terror
(Filmways/Genesis 1971)
RIGHT Audrey Hepburn in Wait Until
Dark (WB-Seven Arts 1967)*

It is Steve who rescues her, frightened and caked in mud from clawing her way out of a claypit. He takes her home. She seems safe at last. She prepares to take a bath. And as she closes the door, we see the tell-tale cowboy boots standing in the corner. They walk towards her . . .

Phew!

Audrey Hepburn was the other blind girl, in *Wait Until Dark* (1967), directed by Terence Young from a script by Robert and Jane-Howard Carrington based on Frederick Knott's play. This story was more convoluted and complex – as might be expected, stemming from a work by Mr "Dial M for Murder" Knott. For me, this was a minor pity, because I prefer my suspense concentrated on basically simple "Get her out of this" lines rather than on too many devious twists and turns; but there were many tingling moments in this movie, nonetheless.

The wide-eyed Miss Hepburn played Susy, wife of a photographer, who had become the unwitting custodian of a musical doll stuffed with heroin which some international smugglers wanted to recover. Most of the drama was played out in Susy's basement apartment in New York's Greenwich Village, and there was a brilliant development when Susy, alone with her telephone cord cut and awaiting the return of the gang, decided to use her handicap as a defensive weapon. Her one advantage in being blind was that she needed no light – and she systematically smashed all the light-bulbs except one in the flat.

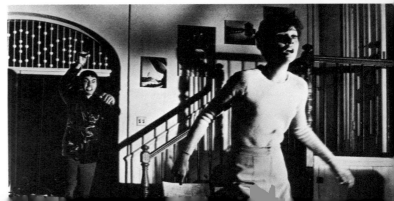

After some internecine murdering, only the master-criminal (Alan Arkin) was left to face her, and he chose a particularly diabolical way of terrorising her into revealing the whereabouts of the drug-doll. He knew that her blindness had been caused by fire after a car crash; and he threatened to set the apartment on fire about her.

But he did not know Susy like we know Susy: she managed to put out the last light and the villain found himself battling in a darkness more familiar to her than to him. A very nice touch – to extract from the handicap which made the victim vulnerable a strength which evened the odds.

When I think of the special terror that comes from the vulnerability of the helpless I am haunted by the shock-memory of two films which, by no means coincidentally, both starred Robert Mitchum.

Now there is an actor who would no doubt have attracted more critical garlands if he had not been so incredibly popular, if he had not tackled such a variety of roles, and if a rugged, sardonic air of self-deprecation did not tend to obscure a high talent.

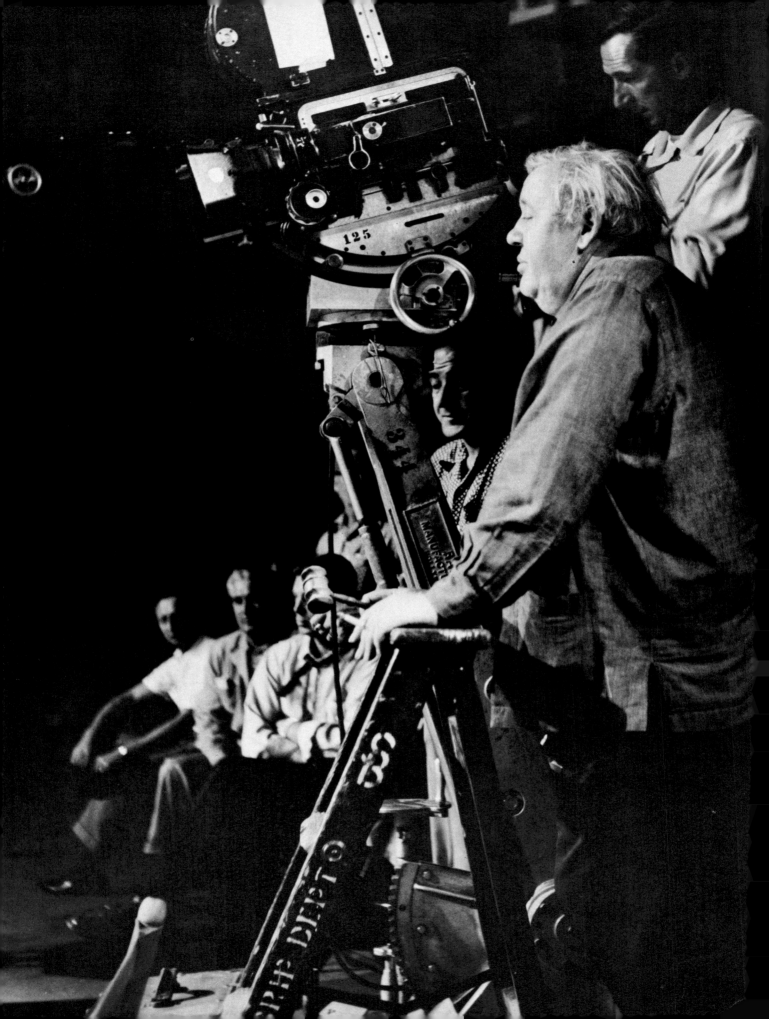

If he had decided to specialise in villains, he might even have come to out-play the great Bogart because, to the menace they both could share, Mitchum was able to add a genuinely frightening brutality.

In 1955 that splendidly theatrical actor Charles Laughton went round to the other side of the cameras to direct Mitchum in *The Night of the Hunter* from James Agee's adaptation of Davis Grubb's novel; and Laughton used every cinematic device of camera-angle, sound and lighting to tighten the tensions. Mitchum played a crazed preacher who married and murdered Shelley Winters for her money – only to find that her small son and daughter had it, and he proceeded relentlessly to hunt them down. Mitchum constructed a really superb characterisation of the obsessed, Biblically-ranting, murderous hellfire preacher, with "love" tattooed on one finger and "hate" on another to point his terrifying parables.

He was, if anything, even more powerful in *Cape Fear* in 1961, possibly because his antagonist this time was the perfectly contrasting Gregory Peck. The film was based on a novel by that very accomplished thriller-writer, John D. McDonald, and was directed in the United States by Britain's J. Lee Thompson with a deceptively languid opening pace which accelerated to a literally shocking climax.

Mitchum played a sex criminal, freed after eight years in prison, who returned to a sleepy little town to terrorise the witness (Gregory Peck) whom he blamed for his conviction. Mitchum uttered no threats, used no violence, broke no laws – and the police were therefore helpless. But his very presence, the tone of his voice, the look in his eyes as he turned them lazily on Peck's attractive wife and adolescent daughter showed with unmistakable and cumulative menace that he would surely take his revenge.

Ultimately Peck planted his wife and daughter on a (as he thought) safely moored houseboat to tempt Mitchum into a trap . . . only to see the boat, its moorings cut, drifting away down-river with his family alone on board with the psychopath. . . .

When the film came to Britain there was a little flurry of controversy because the censor was said to have made a record 161 cuts in it, and Mr Lee Thompson flew here to protest, and the censor then said he had made only 15 cuts. But, whatever the computing, what remained was one of the most powerful suspense films ever made.

LEFT *Charles Laughton turned director for* The Night of the Hunter *(Gregory 1955) starring Robert Mitchum*
BELOW *Mitchum was the menace behind the wheel in* Cape Fear *(Melville-Talbot 1961)*

Loners

PRECEDING PAGES *Robert Ryan finds brief shelter in the desert with Henry Hull (left) in* Inferno *(20th Century-Fox 1953)*
ABOVE *Rhonda Fleming and William Lundigan plot to abandon the injured Robert Ryan in the same film*
RIGHT *Audrey Hepburn throwing petrol around her house in* Wait Until Dark *(WB-Seven Arts 1967)*
OVERLEAF *The famous escape sequence at the climax of* The Anderson Tapes *(Weitman 1971)*

THE ESSENTIAL frailty of characters such as many of those we have just been recalling is their *aloneness*. No one is more isolated at times when communication is a matter of life or death than the person who cannot see or cannot speak, or the child to whom nobody will listen.

The situation of isolation was taken to its extreme in 1953 in a powerful little film called *Inferno*, which had the central character abandoned, injured and utterly alone, in a most inhospitable desert in the middle of nowhere. The film was shot for 3D colour, but appeared towards the end of that transient gimmick boomlet, and most of us saw it "flat". It was directed by Roy Baker from a screenplay by Francis Cockrell.

It seemed at first glance almost as if someone had got hold of a survival manual and set out to dramatise all of its lessons one by one. But there was more to it than that.

The powerful Robert Ryan was a tough, coarse, spoiled and somewhat dissipated millionaire, selfish to the core, who went on a desert expedition to seek manganese with his faithless wife (Rhonda Fleming) and her matchingly worthless boy-friend, William Lundigan. Ryan broke a leg in a fall from his horse, and the other two went off and left him to die.

It seemed a certainty: there was no chance of anyone finding him in that baking desolation, and anyway the lovers could delay a search. He had nothing to eat or drink. He could not even walk a pace. And if this was country where, notoriously, the skilled outdoorsman could not survive, what hope would the hard-drinking, out-of-condition city man have?

The fascination of the development was the way in which all the characteristics which, at the start, had made Ryan so unlikeable gradually became sympathetic and, after a while, we became identified with the tense struggle to survive of this man whom we had begun by disliking and despising. This was some achievement by writer, director and actor. Identification is essential to suspense. You must care about the character to share his dangers, and suspense vanishes the moment the tiny thought enters your mind: "He deserves what he gets." It is easy to identify with the charm of a Cary Grant, the sincerity of a Gregory Peck, for example. But in *Inferno* Ryan had to gather up our sympathy, build our identification, step by painful step with every crisis he overcame.

Even his initial spur to survival was not particularly likeable: a violent urge to live to revenge himself on his wife and her lover. But little by

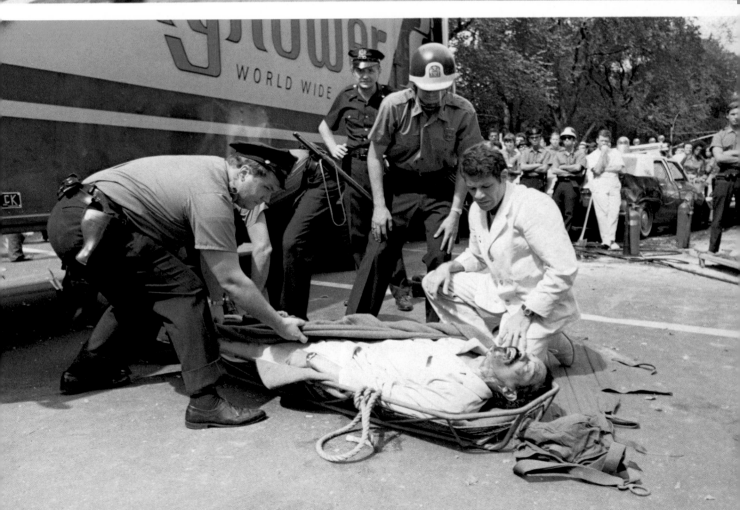

little this melded into a simple determination not to be beaten – either by Nature or by the runaways.

To list all his many ingenuities in keeping life in his body would be to repeat the desert survival manual, but, essentially, he taught himself to set his broken leg in splints made from tent pegs, he agonisingly managed to lower himself in a self-made sort of sling down a precipitous drop to the canyon floor, he learned to extract drinking liquid from apparently barren cactus, he faced a rattle-snake, he killed a rabbit for food – and many a heart missed a beat when his quarry was carried off by a coyote before Ryan could drag his useless leg through the dust to it.

If this sounds like merely a list of incidents, it was more than that. It was suspense through the development of character in action – and it was good stuff.

There was a brave and intelligent twist to the "man alone" theme in an unusually literate thriller which isolated its ambivalent "hero" inside his own destructive personality. This man was not physically isolated as Ryan had been: he was, indeed, at the successful and over-populated heart of Hollywood. He lacked no equipment or resource – except those of self-discipline and trust. The film was nicely titled *In A Lonely Place*, and the lonely place in which he was trapped was his own psyche.

It was made in 1950, directed by Nicholas Ray.

Humphrey Bogart played the leading part, and he was rarely better. No gangster this time, or cop, or private eye. He was a Hollywood writer – tough, irritable, moody, edgy, introspective; his nerve-ends perpetually exposed; living alone with his talent, his reputation and his typewriter: exacerbated rather than fortified by a diet of alcohol and nicotine. His temper was uncontrollable: anything, it seemed, could trigger it; and his violence was more than merely verbal. Perhaps some people thought Bogart over-acted, played this writer like a thug with an outsize chip on his shoulder. No one could think that who had ever lived with an artist through a creative and emotional crisis.

Bogart found himself suspected of a murder that he did not, in fact, commit. He might have been anti-social, but he was no criminal. But the stress within him, reacting to the pressures without,

LEFT *Two scenes from* Don't Look Now *(Casey/Eldorado 1973)*
BELOW *"All in the mind" . . . Humphrey Bogart created tension from within as the star of* In a Lonely Place *(Columbia 1950)*

built up so strongly that his rages, always near boiling point, became explosive. He hit people without good reason. There came a time when he was on the point of murder: in blood-hazed rage, he *could* have killed. One watched the reactions of his friendly and good-looking neighbour, Gloria Grahame, and of his two loyal friends, a policeman and wife played by Frank Lovejoy and Jeff Donnell – utterly stable and controlled (and, frankly, rather dull) in comparison with the violent hair-trigger personality of Bogart. With them, one came to wonder if he was not really a killer after all.

No, he was not. But the thoughtful irony was that you realised that, if circumstances had been only marginally different, he *could* have been a murderer. It was only chance, rather than character, which prevented it. In this man, living alone with a self he could not comprehend, there were the black forces that are inside all of us. The difference was that he could not control them.

Black forces can infect an entire community just as thoroughly as one man, as my favourite handicapped hero, Spencer Tracy, found when he spent a *Bad Day at Black Rock* (1954).

LEFT *Humphrey Bogart spurns help from his friends in* In a Lonely Place *(Columbia 1950)*
ABOVE & BELOW *Spencer Tracey could do with a friend as the stranger in* Bad Day at Black Rock *(MGM 1954)*

Black Rock was a small township in the desert. Transient visitor Tracy was the only outsider there – branded by that fact; handicapped by his white hair and his one arm. Black Rock hid a secret – the secret of how the entire community had become infected by hate and murderous hysteria and had killed a harmless alien and hidden his body. The past was the past: they thought it dead. But it was revived by this imperturbable visitor, probing, questioning, not believing, spying. And, of course, the past was not dead: it was alive in the guilt that all shared and all fermented individually.

Perhaps the suspense may have been weakened by the fact that Spencer Tracy never seemed to show fear. Such was the strength of the man's performance that I never really believed he was in danger – not even from the brutal Robert Ryan (again), with his iron muscles, his black-bushed brows, and his features as though chipped from granite. And once you saw Tracy throw a man across the room with one easy hand and the aid of some judo, you realised that the loss of an arm was not so much of a handicap after all.

Not a blockbuster, but a quiet, slow, steady simmering of suspense in an isolated hamlet where you could sense the hatred festering in the dry sun; and echoing in the mind from the conflict played out between Tracy and Ryan.

Dore Schary produced, John Sturges directed, from a script by Millard Kaufman based on a story by Howard Breslin.

Three more scenes from Bad Day at Black Rock *(MGM 1954) with Spencer Tracey as the one-armed hero*

It's All
in the Mind

PRECEDING PAGES *James Stewart haunted by the dual personalities of Kim*
Novak in Alfred Hitchcock's Vertigo *(Paramount/Hitchcock 1957)*
Psychology was the star but could not overshadow either Ingrid Bergman
(above) *as a doctor in* Spellbound *(Selznick 1945), or Joan Bennett* (right)
as the victim in Secret Beyond the Door *(Universal Int. 1948)*

THE SUSPENSE film that makes fullest use of all that
is now known of the hidden depths of the human
mind has yet to be made. Nonetheless, Hollywood
has several times been unable to resist the temptation to swallow a dose or two of psychiatry ready-
made in the interests of plotting thrills. Usually the
entertainment value has been stronger than the
psychiatric credibility: the latter on the facile over-
simplified level of rent-a-trauma.

Alfred Hitchcock was in there with a harmless
and suspenseful piece of hokum called *Spellbound*
in 1945. The psychiatric window-dressing was
impressive. Ben Hecht, who was fascinated by
psychoanalysis, wrote the screenplay. There was a
psychiatric consultant among the credits. And
surrealist master-painter Salvador Dali was hired
to paint dream sequences.

A very good idea, this. The dreams, the nightmares that we all have are sharp and clear in their
brief and vivid lives – yet the screen convention
had been to fuzz and haze and mist and soften
them. It took Hitchcock to bring to a screen
thriller the bold clarity of Dali-dreams, with their
suggestive distortions and timeless, unending per-
spectives . . . and including (ugh) close-ups of a
pair of scissors at work on an eye.

This was not, incidentally, Salvador Dali's
introduction to the cinema: in 1929 he had colla-
borated in writing *Un Chien Andalou* with the man
whose cinematic imagination has always flowered
in the gardens of the unconscious mind: Luis
Buñuel.

Most of *Spellbound* took place in a mental home,
where Ingrid Bergman was the best-looking doctor
you have ever seen. When Gregory Peck arrived as
the new head doctor, she fell in love with him; but
soon his staring eyes beneath knitted brows, his
long pauses and the heavy shadows surrounding
him led her, like us, to suspect that he was not
"Dr Edwardes" at all, but was really a mental case
himself who had assumed the identity of the doctor.
In that case, what had happened to the real doctor?
Mr Peck could not say, because he was suffering
from amnesia and could not remember his past.
While we began to wonder, he became convinced
that he was a murderer and took flight, sought by
the police. Convinced of his innocence – but
needing to persuade the fugitive to prove it – Ingrid
Bergman caught up with Peck and took him for
shelter to a psychoanalyst, who sought to unravel
the truth in Peck's dreams.

The truth was that Peck was the victim of an

over-neat guilt complex. As a child he had (wrongly) blamed himself for his brother's death in an accident. Years later, he had seen the real Dr Edwardes killed in somewhat similar circumstances. This, too, was an accident. But the traumatic shock of the repeated experience caused Peck to lose his memory, and the deep-seated guilt feelings from childhood caused him to assume the guilt from the doctor's death.

This being a Hitchcock thriller which happened to use psychiatry for its plot, the end was not yet. We learned that the retiring head of the mental home had in fact murdered Dr Edwardes, and there was a final showdown to come before Dr Ingrid Bergman could write a cool prescription for "happy ever after" with a relieved Gregory Peck.

Psychiatry, plus a suggestion of the Bluebeard legend, plus a lot of Gothic glooms, was the essence of *Secret Beyond the Door*, a thriller made by Fritz Lang in 1947 with Michael Redgrave and Joan Bennett.

The situation is the familiar one of the girl who falls in love with and marries a man about whom she knows little, and finds that the home to which he takes her is one of those gloomy mansions which seem to have been built for the mysterious shadows they throw.

She meets there three people whose existence she had not suspected: her husband's sister, who has been running things and wants to carry on (does anyone remember Mrs Danvers in *Rebecca*?); his secretary, who had hoped to marry him, and always wears a scarf round her face to hide scars from a fire; and his rather hostile son, who had no more been mentioned than the fact of a previous marriage.

The husband also has a handy hobby for a melodrama: he has a "collection" of reconstructions of rooms in which murders have been committed. We visit them all except one: this is kept ominously locked.

Is this the room of the first wife, and did her husband murder her? Well, although he too has a guilt complex, he did not kill her. Not loving her, he wished her dead – and blames himself. To get this across, Lang stages an imaginary trial, with the husband as both accuser and accused.

We end up, many shadows later, with Mr Redgrave and Miss Bennett having a showdown in the locked room. He feels mighty like murdering her, and already has the scarf for strangulation in his hands, when she solves the problem with some lightning psychiatry. She gets him to remember that, when he was a child, he felt like killing his

Tippi Hedren, as a safe breaker,
eludes the unsuspecting cleaner in
Marnie *(Hitchcock/Universal Int. 1964)*

author Winston Graham, in 1964. By now the psychological insights were not just surprise gimmicks to unwind a plot as rapidly as an O. Henry short story; nor were they simply plot-props on the level of a lost key or a drawn gun. The childhood roots of Marnie's problem were certainly the fulcrum of the plot; but they were also a vital strand in her character, the main force of her motivation; and the question of if and how they would be uncovered was as much a suspense mystery as that of if and how the police would catch up with her.

For Marnie (Tippi Hedren) was a thief, a compulsive thief. She would take a job in an office, win liking and trust by her good looks, manners and work; then rob the safe and move to another part of the country, changing her wig, her name, her identity.

This was the sequence when she went to work for Sean Connery, a successful businessman; but he replaced the stolen money, tracked her down, and forced her to marry him as the only alternative to being handed over to the police.

mother when she locked him in and went off with a man. Aha, Miss Bennett more or less explains, looking lovely with her dark hair and smouldering eyes and lips. You don't really want to kill *me*: you really want to kill your mother, for whom I'm a psychological substitute. And, far quicker than five years on an analyst's couch at five guineas an hour, Mr Redgrave has an instant insight and is cured.

This is just as well, because they have been too busy with their psychiatry to notice that the jealous secretary has locked the door and set fire to the house. But our hero is not a Freud and rescues his bride.

In a more serious vein, the psychiatric undertones of a suspense story had reached a more realistic level when Alfred Hitchcock came to film *Marnie*, based on the novel by that fine and careful

Marnie had many problems which sprang naturally from character and situation and made up the warp and weft of an extraordinarily engrossing film. Cool, desperately detached, she could find in herself no affection for any living thing except her horse. She was sexually frigid, and when her husband used force, she tried to drown herself. There was a constant threat of recognition by some victim from her past. She was torn by nightmares, and the sight of the colour red – in a vase of flowers, a spot of ink on her white blouse – devastated her.

The uncovering of the springs of her neurosis was utterly convincing and bitterly painful. Marnie had always said she was an orphan, but her husband tracked down her mother and brought the two face to face. There was a beautifully acted scene when Marnie met up again with her mother (Louise Latham), who even now could show no more affection to her daughter than Marnie could to her husband . . . when Marnie watched while this mother lavished her love on a neighbour's child, and Marnie's eyes begged, but in vain, for a morsel of tenderness, as she had begged in vain as a child.

It transpired that the mother had been a prostitute and Marnie, as a small child, had killed a customer with a poker to protect her. The horror had erased the memory from her conscious mind. But, deep in her unconscious, the roots entwined: the fear of sex, the compulsive stealing as some sort of compensation, the inability to trust a human being with her love, the shattering effect of a blood-red colour.

Mercifully for plausibility, there was no lightning transformation. Marnie emerged from the revelations as shattered as anyone except some script-writers of the Forties would expect; but there was hope ahead.

This was not a film in which Hitchcock indulged his flair for spectacularly thrilling set-pieces in dramatic, and often precipitous, situations. But it is memorable, among many things, for the way in which he wrung suspense out of the simplest materials. When Marnie was robbing a safe, for example, while an office cleaner mopped the floor inexorably towards her – no more than that – the heart felt like bursting.

All-American girl Barbara Bel Geddes (above) *and all-American mystery*
Kim Novak (right) *bewildered James Stewart in* Vertigo *(Paramount/ Hitchcock 1957)*

Psychiatric mainsprings to the plot, plus a full quota of powerful shock-pieces, came together when Hitchcock made *Vertigo* in 1958. This was a fascinating film which worked on the audience on several levels: and, even if you did not care to think too much about the murkier aspects of the main characters' ids and egos, you were still left with a rattling good suspense yarn in which surprise exploded tension with stunning frequency.

James Stewart was a San Francisco policeman who had resigned from the force when he lost his head for heights after seeing a colleague fall to his death, and nearly losing his own life at the same time. This was no minor vertigo: looking down from a height was a disintegrating, impossible-to-face situation.

He was hired to keep an eye on an acquaintance's wife Madeleine (Kim Novak), who was said to be neurotic to the point of suicide. She seemed to be obsessed by a Spanish beauty who had killed herself in an earlier life – and in the course of his trailings, Stewart fell heavily in love with her. He saved her from drowning, but his phobia made him powerless to save her when she climbed to the top of a church tower and then threw herself off to her death.

Almighty shock: what on earth is Hitchcock up to, killing off his heroine, a major star like Miss Novak, early in the film? While you are still reeling from this, Stewart, overcome by guilt at his responsibility for Madeleine's death, has a nervous breakdown, through which his hand is metaphorically held by the very antithesis of the neurotic Madeleine: a bright, healthy, chattery, all-American girl (Barbara Bel Geddes). Can she steer him through to love and normality? No, because one day Stewart sees in the street a girl who has an uncanny resemblance to the dead Madeleine. Different coloured hair, different make-up, walk and personality – but in her he sees his dead love. This new girl, Judy, is also played by Kim Novak and the make-up is a brilliant achievement, the

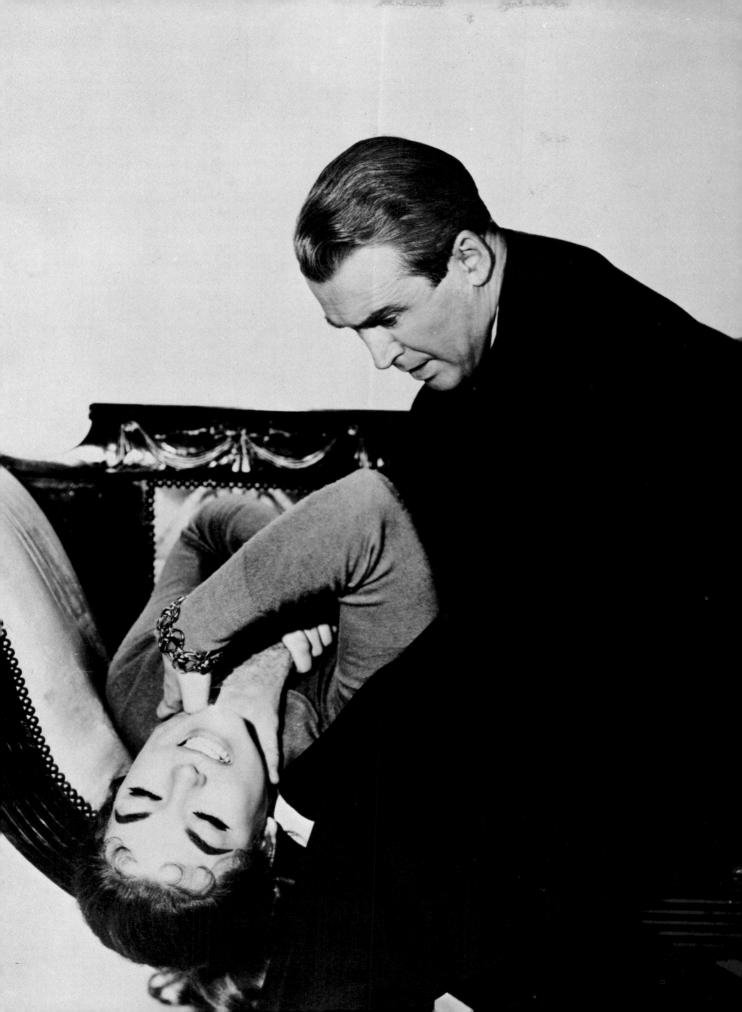

resemblances and the differences between Judy and Madeleine heightening each other. Judy swears she has never met Stewart before, never heard of Madeleine. But the detective becomes obsessed by her; tries to recreate Madeleine in her, persuades her to buy a wig like Madeleine's hair, to wear clothes that Madeleine would have worn.

What we learn, but he doesn't, is that Judy and Madeleine are the same person. The background to this is one of those tortured, punctured pieces of incidental plotting which Hitchcock films so often gloss lightly over and which don't worry you until you leave the cinema and start to think over the story. At the time, you are so fascinated by the Judy/Madeleine double-character hoax, so spellbound by the detective's impossible pursuit of a dead love, so anxious to know if he will discover the truth and what he will do about it, that the intricacies of the incidental sub-plot mercifully pass you by.

What happens is that Judy herself seems to be falling in love with Stewart and he becomes suspicious of her. To try to make her confess, he has not only to confront her with the scene of Madeleine's supposed suicide: he has also to confront his own nightmare. He takes her back to the church tower. He forces himself up the steep wooden stairs to the vertiginous top. He makes her as terrified as he is and – dramatic full circle – he sees her stumble and fall, this time really to her death.

If only for its title, the most successful suspense film ever made belongs here: *Psycho*. Successful not only for the phenomenal box-office takings of a movie produced on a very modest budget; not only for its unparalleled emotional impact on millions of people in audiences all over the world; but successful too as a triumph of the film-maker's skills.

When the film first appeared in 1960, many critics complained about the horrors of the story. Alfred Hitchcock professed surprise: it was a fun film, he maintained. Now, Mr Hitchcock may have a black and bizarre and dry sense of humour, but it seems that in this case it was not critically shared. A lot of printer's ink and a lot of air-time have been devoted to heavy-handed intellectual and psychological analysis of his little film. And perhaps all that he meant was that the pundits were taking it much too seriously.

Psycho was fun – in the sense that the old Grand Guignol theatre was fun. It was no serious casebook study of a psychotic. It was no throbbing revelation of crime and punishment. It was simply a nail-biting sequence of damn good thrills, one

Master mystifier Alfred Hitchcock and Janet Leigh in scenes from Psycho *(Shamley 1960)*

after another, made with stunningly assured technique by a man who was confident that the result would attract and entertain untold millions of people. As it did.

With absolute assurance Hitchcock played with the audience, manipulating and controlling their emotions as a puppet-master controls his marionettes. After a lifetime of suspense films, he knew precisely what response he would get from what effects. He knew when to distribute the red herrings, when to deceive us, when to let us into a secret, when to tighten the screws gradually, when to stun with ferocious shock.

He cheated us outrageously, of course (and how we loved it), positioning his cameras with masterly cunning so as to mislead us into the wrong paths of speculation – with the result that the revelations, when they came, were all the more powerful.

The plot, you will remember, starts with Janet Leigh, involved in a surreptitious love affair, stealing a lot of cash from her employer. On the run with it, she stops for the night at a lonely, gloomy and eerie motel run by Anthony Perkins. He tells her he lives in the even more eerie and run-down Gothic mansion next door with his sick mother. Janet Leigh takes a shower, and is brutally slashed to death by the old woman. No one who saw it will forget the shock effect of that scene. Not only because of its terrifying realism, with the blood gushing and swirling on the shower floor; but also because Miss Leigh was a sympathetic and star figure. Although she had stolen, we felt involved

ABOVE & BELOW *The eyes have it;
terrorized and terrorizer in* Psycho
(Shamley 1960)
RIGHT *Andy Robinson as another
psychopathic killer at bay with a
hostage in* Dirty Harry *(WB/Malpaso
1971)*
OVERLEAF *Burt Reynolds takes a truck-top leap in*
Shamus *(Columbia/Weitman 1972)*

with her (as we were involved with Marnie); we wanted her to get away; and here, with two-thirds of the film still to go, we watched helplessly as the life and the beauty and the hopes were butchered out of her.

We saw Anthony Perkins, distraught, cleaning up and disposing of her body in a lake; and, as three people began to investigate, our sympathies were subtly manoeuvred to the good-looking young man who, it seemed, must try to protect a homicidal mother. We saw the mother stab to death a probing detective – all the more terrifying because we watched the horror in Martin Balsam's eyes as the knife descended. We heard Perkins talking with his mother; saw him carry her down to a hideout in the cellar. And then we learned that the mother had been dead for years!

The explanation, of course was that Perkins (who indulged in the shuddery pastime of taxidermy) was a psychotic schizophrenic, who murdered when he wore the persona, as well as the clothes, of his dead mother.

A dozen times or more we were "cheated" unconscionably so that we believed the murderous old harridan was living and breathing and talking – and slaying. But it didn't matter. All quibbles of plot were overwhelmed in the exploding catharsis of shock.

This, above all others, was a suspense film contrived purely for suspense's sake.

LEFT *Two scenes from* Bullitt *(Solar 1968) starring Steve McQueen*
BELOW *Before the terror began. Janet Leigh in an early scene from* Psycho *(Shamley 1960)*

Hey Presto!
Mr Welles!

PRECEDING PAGES *Orson Welles as black marketeer in* The Third Man
*(London Films 1949) and as tycoon (*above & right*) in* Citizen Kane
(Mercury 1941)

ONE DAY when I was a literary agent, picking a wary path through the golden minefields of film deals, a phone call came through from Rome. A briskly pleasant voice said she was Mr Orson Welles's secretary; Mr Welles had just read a very new thriller that I was handling and wanted to buy an option on the movie rights.

The book was a suspense story of quiet quality in which I had a great deal of faith, but in which I had been unable to interest Hollywood because the author's name was not exactly a household word: the quality of the story mattered less to most producers than the ready-made publicity of a best-selling "big name". Because I believed in the book, I did not want to sell an option, which would have tied up the rights for a year in exchange for only ten per cent of an ultimate price: I wanted an outright sale, so that the full price would be paid as soon as possible.

I said as much to the secretary. She said Mr Welles was sorry: he would only buy an option. I said in that case I would like to discuss it with Mr Welles. She was still sorry, but Mr Welles was not available.

We batted about like this for a few minutes, the lady insisting on an option or nothing, I insisting on an outright sale. Suddenly, without even a warning click, the deeply resonant familiar voice of Orson Welles broke into the conversation. "Mr Hammond? I have been listening to your discussion. I want to buy the film rights to this book. What is your price?"

I told him.

"No option?"

"No option."

"An outright sale?"

"An outright sale."

"All right, then. Be in touch with my lawyers and draw up the contract. Good day to you."

He signed the contract. He paid the money. So far as I know, he never made the film.

There is a lot of Orson Welles in that minor reminiscence – not least, incidentally, the openness. Some film men of international fame try to hide their identities, in the hope that they will acquire movie rights more cheaply – and to the author's loss – if they get a nominee to do the purchasing for them.

There is Welles the joker and the man who cannot resist a theatrical touch, in listening in silently on another line and then breaking in potently at the psychological moment of impasse to clinch the deal in a few moments. There is Welles the artist/impresario, who can spot and value talent and does not need the ballyhoo of a big name attached to give confidence to his judgment. There is Welles the film-maker of outstanding achievement but even more prolific ambition, whose career is strewn with unrealised projects. And there is the other side of the coin to the Orson Welles whose bold and revolutionary genius injected art into the cinema: the Welles who quite simply loves a good suspense film.

This is not the place to add to the endless and justified paeans of analytical praise for *Citizen Kane* and *The Magnificent Ambersons*, for example – even though many of their techniques have since enriched the more commercial world of the suspense cinema. But no retrospective survey of suspense films should neglect the contributions of Orson Welles, flawed though some of them might have been – in that case, splendidly flawed – because individual scenes of the authentic Wellesian savour stand out unshakeably in the memory like peaks from the plain, when their contexts have been lost in the blur of time and derivation.

Orson Welles's first explosion into the commercial cinema was very nearly in the suspense genre. When he went to Hollywood in 1939 he was to film an adaptation of Conrad's *Heart of Darkness* (in which, incidentally, seven years before Robert Montgomery's *The Lady in the Lake*, he planned to use the camera subjectively, as a main character). Then he was asked if, first, he would make a film version of the Nicholas Blake thriller, *The Smiler with the Knife*. A script was prepared, but Welles could not get the stars he wanted – so he did not make *The Smiler with the Knife*.

A script was also written for *Heart of Darkness*, test scenes were shot, Welles grew a beard – but, for a variety of reasons, this film was not made either.

Instead, Welles made *Citizen Kane* – and history.

After that, there was to be a spy suspense story, *The Way to Santiago*, in 1941. It was to be set in Mexico, with Welles as an Allied agent saved from Nazis by his spy girl-friend. Again Welles worked on the script; again the film was never made.

But in 1942–43 he produced, part-directed, co-scripted and acted in a splendid diversion in suspense based on Eric Ambler's novel *Journey Into Fear*. This was a spy thriller set in the wartime Near East, about an innocent American engineer (Joseph Cotten), pursued by Nazi agents and blundering from danger to danger without seeming to know too much of what it was all about.

It was essentially a hunter-and-hunted story, with settings that were often seedy but always exotic. The opening was in Istanbul, the climax in Batum, and all the terrors between were crammed claustrophobically between the low ceilings and narrow partitions of a scruffy little steamer ploughing the Black Sea. There, to the suspensery of the confined space, flickering with uneven light, throbbing with rackety engines, peopled by a dozen disparate characters thrown up by the war, Welles added a dramatic ingredient: one of the passengers was the bizarre paid assassin (*see Chapter 3*) who sat in his tiny cabin, obsessively playing his scratched and cracked gramophone record over and over again, to emerge like a myopic black beetle scuttling down the narrow companionways in pursuit of his prey, the naive Mr Cotten, in whose peril nobody else would believe.

One of the most sinister parts of this killer's characterisation was that he never spoke; and this, it would seem, is one of those examples of brilliance striking from expediency. Jack Moss, who played the villain, was in fact Orson Welles's manager. He had never acted on screen – and he agreed to do the part only on condition that he had no lines to say.

The other overwhelming character in the whole film, of course (even though his screen time was comparatively short), was Orson Welles himself as Colonel Haki, head of the Turkish Secret Police.

Anne Baxter, Joseph Cotten and Tim Holt starred in Welles' tantalizing masterpiece The Magnificent Ambersons *(Mercury 1942)*

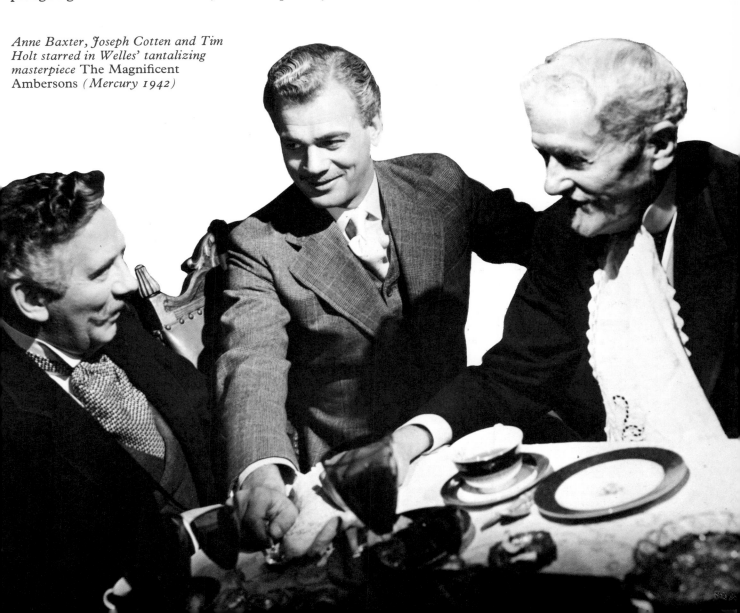

Massive in astrakhan hat and ankle length fur-collared greatcoat, he gave himself lines of superb theatricality which might have been ham if delivered by a less confident actor or one with less of the magic instinct for timing.

Journey Into Fear lives for its portrait gallery, its atmosphere, and for two set-pieces in particular. One reflected Welles's boyhood interest in conjuring and stage magic, an interest said to have been fostered by Houdini himself.

Early in the film, Joseph Cotten was taken to a tatty nightclub in Istanbul, where a stage magician announced an act involving a wooden cross and a coffin. He picked on the unwilling American from

the audience as his stooge. Cotten, feebly protesting but too embarrassed to break away, was tied to the cross. The magician started to get into the coffin – and, just as the lights were killed, we saw the insect-like assassin sidling into the room. The lights came up . . . and everything seemed to happen at once. Our eyes began to take in the fact that Cotten and the magician had switched places . . . a woman screamed . . . a shot crashed out . . . the magician was slumped dead on the cross, blood seeping from his wound . . . Cotten was clambering unhurt out of the coffin. The conjuror's switch in the brief darkness had meant that the killer's bullet had found the wrong body.

The climax of the film was set in Batum, where Cotten, the Secret Police chief and the assassin played out for the last time the "Who shall live, who shall die?" question on the narrow ledges outside the hotel, high above the upturned faces of watchers goggling from the street. Rain was falling in a blinding downpour. On the slippery, washed ledges the three edged precariously, murderously, round the treacherous pillars, beneath flapping streaming awnings, the killer with a gun in one hand, the other dabbing feverishly at the thick pebble lenses of his glasses which were filmed with rain and destroying his vision. The police chief was wounded; the killer's last bullet was fired. He hurled the gun at Cotten, then tried to push him from the ledge.

But let's not prolong the agony: the assassin it was who slipped – and died.

It was in 1946 that Orson Welles was next tempted on to the slippery slopes of suspense. At least, that was the year in which he made *The Lady from Shanghai*, but it was not until 1948 that cinemagoers were able to see it. The studio bosses were so bothered by many things in the film – not least the bewilderments of the plot and the fact that it made a star, Rita Hayworth, into a murderess and, adding insult to image-injury, left her to die in the last reel – that they held up distribution for nearly two years. It would seem that audiences agreed with them, because commercially the film was a flop. But it is packed with moments of appeal to the cinephile.

*Orson Welles, as actor (*right*), dominates Everett Sloane and, as director (*above*), builds the tension between Joseph Cotten and Jack Moss in* Journey into Fear *(Mercury 1942)*

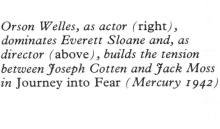

After all, you do not go to an Orson Welles movie to see a nice simple little plot and a burnishing of the image of a happy-ever-after star. You go to see theatrically heightened characters locked in conflict against colourful and unusual settings, lighted and scored imaginatively, photographed boldly, and the whole thing peppered with unexpected details of surprise that a wiser and duller director would either eschew or not think of in the first place.

As usual, as well as directing, Welles wrote the script of *The Lady from Shanghai* (based rather loosely on a novel by Sherwood King), and he also played the hero – a young Irish seaman who had knocked about the world and seen its evil, but still retained his clear-eyed trust in the goodness of others. Unfortunately for him, he reposed this trust in Rita Hayworth, whose cool good looks concealed a murky past and murderous inclinations for the future. She was married, lovelessly, to a waspish, impotent, crippled advocate, acted like a malevolent lizard by the brilliant Everett Sloane. As a result of a plot whose complexities nobody (including, one suspects, Mr Welles) understood, our hero signed a confession to a murder which he thought was a hoax but which turned out to be all too real. Put on trial, he was defended by Everett Sloane, who was determined to lose the case and

Scenes from The Lady from Shanghai *(Columbia 1948) starring Orson Welles, Rita Hayworth and Everett Sloane*

enjoy seeing his client executed. Before the inevitable happened, Welles escaped – to a final triangular showdown in a hall of mirrors, which has become one of the classic scenes of the post-war cinema, and to which we shall return in a moment.

One is apt to forget that, with all the resonant theatricality of Orson Welles, there is a youthful romanticism underlying it all, and this quality came into exuberant play in *The Lady from Shanghai*. Perhaps this has never been more marked than in the long sequences where the main characters took a yacht cruise to San Francisco (for which Welles borrowed Errol Flynn's craft, *Circe*). The camera seemed almost to caress Rita Hayworth as the sun played with her hair and her long limbs while she playfully teased the young seaman into her web – and while her crippled husband squeezed elliptical dialogue out of a body wracked by pain and his guest-partner-victim jerkily, jokily, neurotically worried about the atomic end of the world.

Welles did not miss a chance throughout the whole film to counterpoint the words and actions with visual detail which enriched the texture and heightened the atmosphere. When the lovers met secretly and Rita Hayworth read aloud the fake murder confession, he staged the scene in the chiaroscuro light and echoing chambers of an aquarium. The ambivalent lovers almost in silhouette; the light coming from the watery tanks where, behind them, eerie creatures from the depths of the sea and of time writhed and glided and had their implacable being, in parallel to the monstrous instincts which writhed in the depths of the human psyche. Welles matched his shots with the characters, so that when Rita Hayworth described the murder a shark appeared behind her silhouette; when she spoke of her husband, a conger eel.

When the hero escaped from the courtroom, Welles led him into bizarre set-ups in quick succession so that the feeling of nightmare began to scream in the mind. First he hid in a Chinese theatre, the unfamiliar music jangling and scraping and squeaking, the actors' stylised make-up adding unreality, their mask-like appearance not quite concealing their realisation that there was one non-Chinese face in the audience.

Then he was pursued to an empty funfair, into one of those crazy houses of terror, where madness and hell were made manifest as he hurtled giddily down huge slides, through trapdoors, into and beyond the very gaping mouths of gigantic model dragons. Your stomach heaved and your nerves tore as you were dragged right into the action – and

to be sure this was so, it was photographed by a camera crew sliding prostrate with the camera on a mat through the whole helter-skelter.

And so to that unforgettable climax, which justified the whole film, in the mirror maze. There Welles heard Rita Hayworth confess to murder; there they were both confronted by her crippled husband. Reality and unreality, truth and lies, dream and nightmare were all explicit in the endlessly repeated reflections; the beauty of the woman haunting, the vindictiveness of the cripple taunting, both multiplied a thousand thousand times to an ever-receding infinity. Which was the substance, which the false image? Just as the Welles-character had been unable to know in the almighty double-cross they had made of his life, so he could not tell now. Nor could the husband and wife as they drew guns and blazed away at each other. Mirrors shattered, splintered glass flew, images vanished, until it was the flesh and not the image which took the bullets, and husband and wife shot each other, and the reality which remained was evil and the evil died.

At least, the husband died. Miss Hayworth was merely dying slowly enough to permit her to speak some lines of such embarrassing theatricality that it was no wonder her lover left her to it and walked out to regain the sunlight and his innocence.

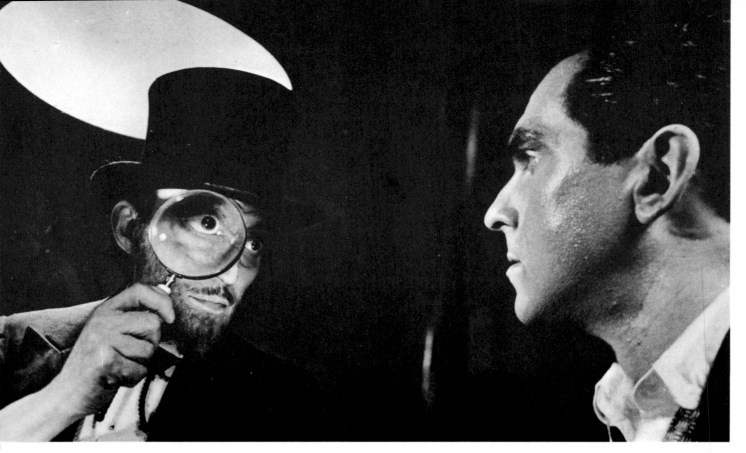

Orson Welles was Gregory Arkadin (below), Michael Redgrave was Burgomil Trebitsch and Mischa Auer was the professor (above) in Confidential Report *(Sevilla Studios – Mercury 1955)*
RIGHT *A tense moment in Welles'* The Third Man *(London Films 1949)*

It is tempting to leave him there, but before the endcredits roll to this story of Orson Welles's excursions into suspense, time should be made for a glance at a film which had an extraordinarily mixed reception, even for him. It was made in 1954 under Welles's own title of *Mr Arkadin*, was shown in Britain a year later as *Confidential Report*, and was not shown in the US until 1962, by which time it had re-acquired its original title.

A lot of European critics saw a lot that was very good in the film; a lot of the Americans thought it was simply awful. I suspect that at the root of many of the attacks on *Mr Arkadin* is the old critical posture of attacking a work for not being what it was never intended to be.

Mr Arkadin and *Citizen Kane* were both, in simplest terms, about the search to uncover the past of a tycoon. There the resemblance ends. But many earnest and worthy students have attacked the baroque, theatrical, deliberately unreal *Arkadin* for not being the revolutionary genius of *Kane*. Foolish fellows. If they relaxed and regarded *Arkadin* merely as a highly-coloured, larger-than-life, more-exciting-than-life piece of entertaining suspense, the conjuring by a rumbustious magician of a gallery of characters to make an actor's mouth water, they would see in it much to savour.

Welles directed, Welles scripted, Welles was the art director, Welles designed the costumes, Welles was the narrator – and you can guess who played the massive, spade-bearded, towering tycoon character of Gregory Arkadin.

The story was basically about Arkadin hiring a young American to uncover forgotten events in his early life. Only later did the American realise that, as he tracked down the people who knew the secrets of Arkadin's hidden past, the financier was having them murdered one by one, and intended at the end to have his own investigator murdered too so that the trail he had uncovered would be obliterated for ever.

But all this was simply a thread on which to hang the ornate jewels of those characters. Mischa Auer, the tall, cadaverous, top-hatted, impoverished Russian owner of a Copenhagen flea circus, sitting alone in a tiny room with the loathsome insects which are the only creatures for which he cares, feeding them on his own scrawny arm, peering with huge distorted eye through a large magnifying glass at the probing investigator.

Akim Tamiroff, starving in Munich as a scruffy unshaven beggar; clinging to his black bowler hat, his steel-rimmed glasses, his ragged muffler; lying back on a pallet in long woollen underpants and willing to trade his secrets for a meal.

Katina Paxinou, card-playing, chain-smoking, the ruthless woman who had run a criminal gang in Europe and now lived on her fortune in Mexico. And Michael Redgrave, an ineffectual dealer, scrabbling about his shop crammed with antique junk, wearing a dressing-gown and hairnet and clutching his kittens.

Such characters simmer the suspense of which entertainment is made.

Alas, despite all the films which bear on every sound and sequence the characteristic stamp of Orson Welles, I suspect that many people still remember him best as Harry Lime in *The Third Man* (1949), which Graham Greene wrote and Carol Reed directed. It was, to my mind, the first British post-war suspense film to achieve outstanding quality. Story – set against the black market operations of Allied-occupied Vienna – acting, directing were all flawless. And the voice and the face which stay longest in the memory are those of Orson Welles/Harry Lime, pursued through the sewers or sitting high on the fairground wheel and talking about the Swiss and their cuckoo clock.

In character to the end . . . Welles hated the part.

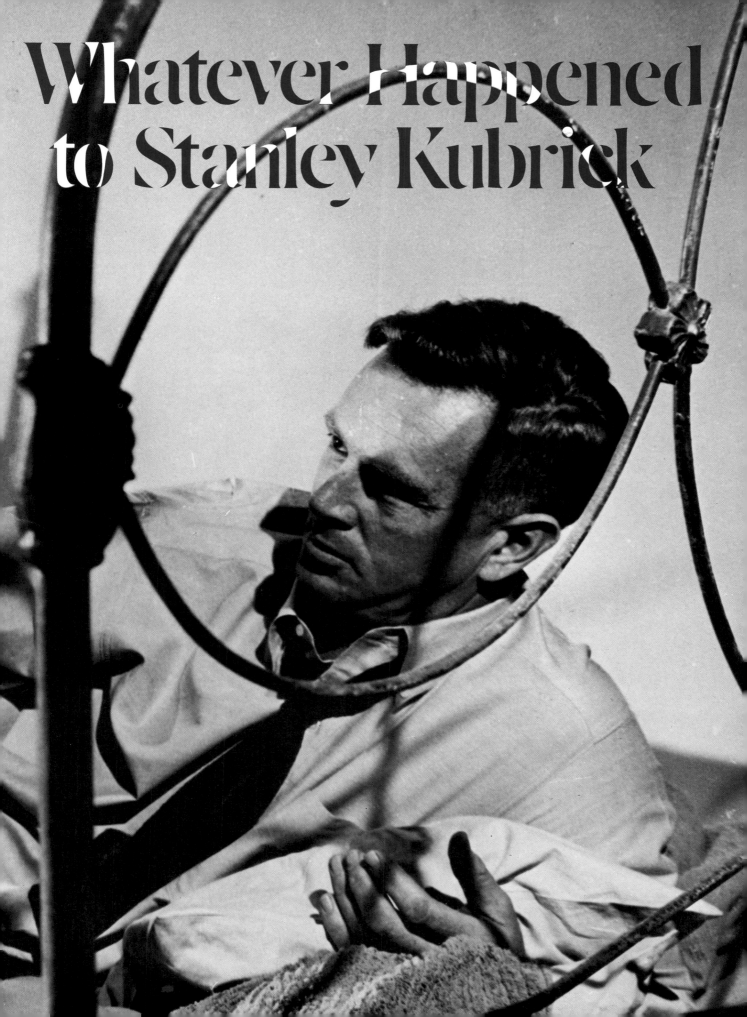

Whatever Happened to Stanley Kubrick

WHO'S THAT again? Kubrick? The man described as the cinema's greatest perfectionist; hailed in America as one of the world's three most important film-makers (alongside Europe's Bergman and Fellini)? The man who chuckled at and with the nymphet theme when he directed *Lolita*; who produced chilling, thoughtful laughter at the end of the world when he produced, directed and co-scripted *Dr Strangelove*; who wove realms of mystic, futuristic space fantasy in fulfilling the same roles with *2001: A Space Odyssey*; and who in *A Clockwork Orange* (1971) produced, directed and scripted a film described often as the sociological masterpiece of the decade and often as dangerously vicious – a film with more violent sex and thuggery per reel than any other I can remember, a film which daringly brought to larger-than-life those areas of the unconscious mind which some people felt were best left hidden.

PRECEDING PAGES *A skilful and entertaining suspense movie,* The Killing *(Harris-Kubrick 1956) starred Sterling Hayden and Marie Windsor*
ABOVE & BELOW *Sue Lyon and James Mason in Kubrick's* Lolita *(Seven Arts/Anya/Transworld 1961)*
RIGHT *Paul Newman, up to his thighs in water and up to his neck in trouble in* The Mackintosh Man *(Newman-Foreman/Huston 1973)*
OVERLEAF *Ryan O'Neal, inappropriately clad, stealing the jewels in* The Thief Who Came to Dinner *(Tandem 1973)*

What's Stanley Kubrick doing in a book about suspense movies – towering director of the Seventies though he may be? I'll tell you.

In 1955 a young man, who had produced a couple of 35mm. shorts and a feature which were so little known that they were never even shown in Britain, made a suspense thriller. From the fact that he co-produced it, wrote it, directed it and did the photography and editing himself you may deduce that he had more talent than backing. The movie was called *Killer's Kiss*, and the multitalented man who made it was the young Stanley Kubrick.

LEFT *Frank Sinatra in* The Naked Runner *(Artanis Enterprises 1967)*
ABOVE & BELOW *Peter Sellers starred in Kubrick's* Dr. Strangelove *(Hawk Films 1963)*

Even if one resists the simple critical seductions of hindsight, it is a fascinating movie to look back on in the light of his later stunners. And it is more than that: it is a notable thriller in its own right.

Killer's Kiss shows signs of its modest background in things like erratic lighting, which sometimes does not match up in consecutive scenes. The camera work, unlike many "first" suspense films, resists the temptation to lean heavily on the atmospheric angles of the arty-in-inverted-commas German cinema; nor is it used as a protagonist in the Orson Welles manner. It is used in a smoothly flowing and straightforward style, and when there is an "effect" shot – a face seen through a close-up of a fishbowl, for example – its rarity makes the point without fuss.

The overall style of the film is almost literary in its storytelling: as Kubrick acknowledged in an interview years later, movies have always been to him essentially picture-stories. It is all told in flashback, while the narrator is waiting – Why? For whom? – alone on a railway station. A technique as old and honourable as that of the first cave-man who sat by a fire and told a tale for his supper. But, perhaps because Kubrick lacked the sureness of narrative touch in contriving naturally-evolving climaxes that he developed later, there are other flashbacks, two or three of them, within the overall flashback.

It is a film about lonely people; alone people, which is not quite the same thing; their roots almost

severed from a past which was once good and is now lost; solitary in the impartial big city; at the end of the line.

It starts with a confident, quiet slowness that few directors would dare in the frenetic Seventies. It takes its time to develop, and for nearly half the film you can't guess what the plot is going to be. But this carefully measured leisure gives you a deep feeling for the characters and their context that leaves you, even after all the suspense, with an overwhelming feeling of the humanity of the movie.

This is one of the dimensions that for me has always stamped the suspense film of quality. This is the dimension which has today gone out of fashion: a dimension which I, for one, have found gradually diminishing in Mr Kubrick's films as his technical mastery has increased so that, while I can acknowledge its milestone achievement, I found *A Clockwork Orange*, for example, shockingly un-human.

The peaceful and the violent Kubrick;
LEFT *Tranquility in* 2001; A Space Odyssey *(MGM 1968)*
ABOVE & BELOW *Violence in* A Clockwork Orange *(WB/Polaris 1971)*

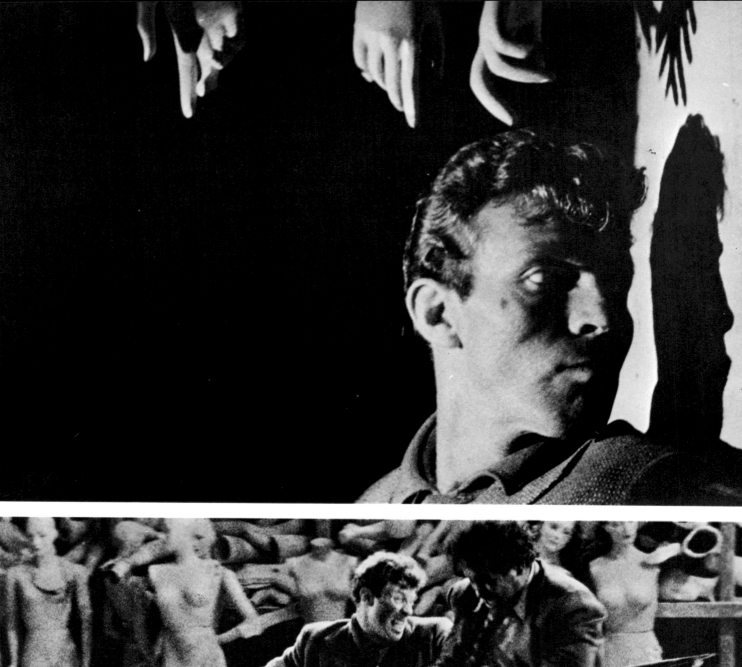

*Jamie Smith (above left) lies in wait and then battles it out with Frank
Silvera (below left) in* Killer's Kiss *(Kubrick/Minotaur 1955)*
ABOVE *The rape scene from* A Clockwork Orange *(WB/Polaris 1971)*

But back to *Killer's Kiss*. The narrator, Davy
Gordon (Jamie Smith) is a young and fading boxer,
past it, but not defeated in his heart. The girl Gloria
(Irene Kane), who lives in the same apartment
block, has, like him, no family nor friends. She's
come down to working as a dance partner in a tatty
hall run by a baddie called Rapallo (Frank Silvera).
Kubrick slowly, movingly, shows the two principals
taking the downgrade: Davy fighting a losing bout
in the ring while Gloria is trying to push off some
heavy passes from Rapallo.

Even he, Rapallo, is made human, understandable. When he stands in his shadowed office,
making up his mind to some mayhem, his eyes fall
on cosy family photographs in nice domestic frames
that he takes the trouble to keep there; and, when
his mind is made up, he gestures irritably, guiltily,
as if knowing he's letting them down and trying
weakly to brush aside their silent reproaches.

The whole story is condensed into three days.
Yet it seems to have the natural, inevitable pace of
real life; and the moments briefly taken out for
little touches of New York street scenes add to the
reality and place it in a context of truth.

Very little violence is actually shown (and what a

change, again, from *A Clockwork Orange*) except in
Davy's boxing match which, in just a few minutes,
gives a better feeling than most movies of what it's
like to lose a fight in the ring. But, in spite of all,
you're on the edge of your seat and you're glad to
be there.

Gloria leaves her job, gets roughed up and
threatened by Rapallo. Davy falls gently in love
with her and, though she suspects his feeling is one
of pity rather than love, she agrees to go on holiday
back in Seattle with him.

She has to return to her dance hall to collect her
pay. Davy waits outside to meet his manager, who's
bringing his fight payoff. Then, while you're
wondering what Rapallo is going to do to stop the
lovers – and knowing only that, whatever it is, it
will be nasty – Kubrick shows that already he was
aware of a powerful but little-used secret of
suspense: the tiny boundary that divides playful-
ness from terror.

This, of course, was one of the dominant and
terrifying techniques of *A Clockwork Orange*, epito-
mised in the scene where Alex and the Droogs
cripple a writer and rape his wife in rhythm to a few
tuneful choruses of "Singin' in the Rain".

137

In *Killer's Kiss* it is a couple of playful drunks who appear, at first sight irrelevantly. But while you wonder, they gleefully snatch Davy's scarf and reel off with it; and, good-humouredly, he chases after them. And he's not there, he's happily and cheerfully absent, when his manager turns up and stands waiting beside Gloria, neither knowing the other's identity; and when Rapallo's thugs, mistaking the manager for Davy, take him up an alley and kill him (and you do not, repeat not, see the actual killing; but you're in no doubt about it; nobody had to spell out the blood in clots in those days). And by the time Davy is back on the scene, he is wanted for the murder, and his girl is a prisoner in an old warehouse.

In the inevitable rescue by Davy there is a classic chase over the rooftops, but even here there are human touches that kill cliché. These villains are not supermen, any more than Davy is: they can stumble on a fire escape, and not for laughs; one of them can fall as you or I would fall and drop out with a twisted ankle.

The suspense is not lessened by these touches: it is increased, because it is more real, seems less contrived.

What is contrived – and brilliantly so – is the climactic set-piece. Rapallo, alone now, pursues Davy into a workshop given over to making window-dressing dummies. A setting to make Alfred Hitchcock's mouth water. Everywhere in the half-light are the naked wax models: bodies, yet not human. Here, decapitated heads lacking a body. There, hands, unattached, lifelessly beckoning, feeling, failing. And in this setting Rapallo, with an axe, fights it out with Davy, with a window pole.

Of course, Davy wins, and here we are back on the railway station where it all began with Davy telling us about it. But we still don't know why he's there, even though a quick look at the clock tells us there are only two minutes to go to the ice-cream. Is he on the run? Is he waiting to be arrested for Rapallo's death? Or the manager's? And what happened to Gloria?

In just a few lines of dialogue Kubrick commits the major weakness of the whole film. Davy has such a headlong rush to wrap up the plot in a dead-pan explanation to us that it's almost laughable: Rapallo's killing was self-defence; his thugs are held for killing the manager; Gloria has been freed. It is too neat, too far from life, in contrast to all that has gone before. But it enables us to be left with a question to the very end, and that is what suspense is all about.

What the hell happened to Gloria, and does she love the guy after all? Yes, of course she does; and, just as Davy turns hopelessly to get his train, here she comes hurrying to him, in time for a long kiss.

Forget the ending: *Killer's Kiss* was a first-class suspense film that foreshadowed awarenesses and techniques that Kubrick was to take to the limit in later years. And, after all, the ending was fair enough for the Fifties. In the Seventies, Gloria would probably have got raped by the railway porter, and there'd have been a lot of unlovely detail and no suspense at all.

The formidably promising talent shown in *Killer's Kiss* helped to secure for Stanley Kubrick studio backing for his next straight thriller, *The Killing*, made in 1956.

This was a much more "professional" job than its forerunner. As well as directing, Kubrick wrote the screenplay from Lionel White's novel, *Clean Break*; he had additional dialogue – very good, too – written by Jim Thompson, and the photography was by the expert Lucien Ballard. He also had the casting of a bunch of actors so experienced in the "character" parts that as soon as they came into camera view you recognised them from a score of Hollywood movies. In few, however, have they produced the acting detail that Kubrick got out of them.

In spite of that extra professionalism – or perhaps because of it – *The Killing* lacks for me the dimension of humanity of its predecessor. It reminded me of one of those documentaries that give you every conceivable fact with immaculate accuracy and leave you without the heart of the truth. This has something to do with the style of the storytelling. Once again there is a narrator; only instead of a lonely failure with blood in his veins, this one sounds like a "March of Time" commentator: strident, confident, detached: "At 4.23 on the afternoon of March 21st, Johnny Clay kept an appointment. . . . Meanwhile, on the other side of the city, George Peatty had a problem at 4.27. . . ."-type thing.

But all the same, *The Killing* was one of the most skilful and entertaining suspense movies of the Fifties. It mesmerised like a ticking time bomb, and every few minutes, with sure craft, Kubrick notched up a new peak of suspense. And all with very little violence, again, though with the obligatory sudden death.

There was no doubt about the relevance of the title. Its tough-slang pun referred not only to the deaths that occurred, but also, much more, to the huge robbery that was to clean-up the takings at a racetrack.

No leisurely opening here. Not a second is wasted. The film opens on the horses preparing for the off at the track and, even before the titles end, the dramatic music has started building the tension. And then, suddenly, as "they're off", the film is off, its plot as headlong as the horses.

One by one we are introduced to the characters as that metallic narrator ticks off the days, the hours, the minutes. Once again, we don't know for a while what the plot is going to be; but this one uses the time to build the mystery and tension rather than to deepen the characters.

They are a more stereotyped lot. Johnny Clay (a performance of great strength from Sterling Hayden, whom Kubrick was to use again years later as the paranoid US Air Force general in *Dr Strangelove*) is a convict just out from five years in Alcatraz, master-minding the two million dollar hold-up. He collects (how, we are never told) a bunch of flawed human beings to fit, like jigsaw pieces, into the intricacy of his plan. There's an Irish barman, an amiable old book-keeper, a tough crooked cop; and there's little George Peatty, played by Elisha Cook Jr – he of the bulging eyes and mobile mouth; here the incarnation of fear and uncertainty and in countless other Hollywood thrillers the personification of the staring-eyed boy killer. (Even Humphrey Bogart, you may remember, in other places, had to take our Elisha's gun away from him a time or two.)

Kubrick plays tricks with time as his characters become enmeshed in the plot. He takes each of them and plays his incident through to the next turn of the screw; then goes back to an earlier moment in time to see what somebody else was doing.

Even the incidental small parts have "character" stamped right through them. The marksman hired to shoot a winning racehorse to cause a diversion from the robbery is a war veteran with deformed speech that comes through teeth fixed in a rictus rigidity. The old retired wrestler, who picks a fight with the police to create another diversion, spends his spare time in a parlour where old men pay to hire chessboards, and he philosophises in heavy Mittel-European with reflections like "The gangster and the artist are the same in the eyes of the masses."

If *Killer's Kiss* had one big dramatic set-piece, *The Killing* has a score of small dramatic touches to heighten the irony and the tension. When the marksman is himself shot dead, his limp hand flops beside a horseshoe which has just been given him "for luck" by a Negro whom he insulted. Sterling Hayden's sub machine-gun is concealed in a

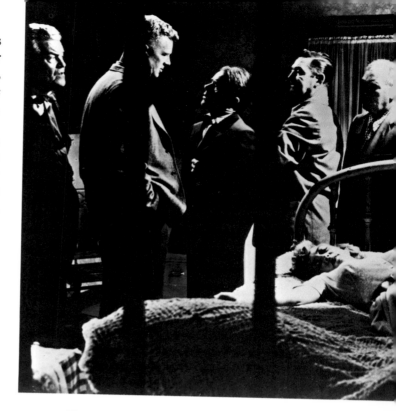

Two scenes from Stanley Kubrick's
The Killing *(Harris/Kubrick 1956)*

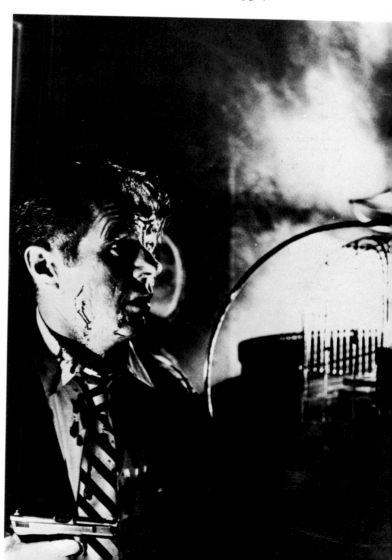

presentation box of roses. For the robbery he
disguises himself with a grotesque rubber mask,
clown-like, sinister in its incongruity (just as the
young thugs in *A Clockwork Orange* disguised
themselves with masks with hugely elongated noses
when they went on their sex-and-blood forays).
When George Peatty shoots his sluttish wife who
has betrayed the robbery plan, he does it in the
presence of a parrot talking unintelligently in its
cage; and when George falls dead from an earlier
wound, he brings down the cage, with squawking
bird, to give Kubrick a chance for some really
effective camera angles.

After *A Clockwork Orange*, when Kubrick was
talking about his philosophy of film-making, he
said: "I always revert to E. M. Forster's 'Aspects
of the Novel', where he tells about the first caveman
telling his friends a story as they sit around a fire.
They either fell asleep, threw a rock at him or
listened. The problem obviously is you've got to
make people pay attention long enough to get across
what you've got to say. . . . It comes back to it somehow, by narrative or surprise or whatever it is, that
you've got to keep the audience's interest for more
than 15 or 20 minutes, which is about as long as
you can keep it if no narrative or major character
interest develops."

In *The Killing* he didn't wait 15 or 20 minutes: it
seemed that there was a new development to height-
en the tension, a new question, every five minutes

at most. Will the heavy police guards foil the
robbery? No. So will the innocent bystanders who
interrupt? No. So maybe the book-keeper will
when he turns up drunk?

Then, when the raid succeeds, will Hayden
abandon his confederates and abscond with the
loot? No. But will the cheap crook to whom the
plot has been betrayed get it? He has a good
murderous try, but Hayden escapes even this.

He buys a cheap secondhand suitcase for his two
million stolen dollars. But the lock doesn't catch
properly. . . . The airline will, won't, will, no they
won't let him take it in the cabin with him. By now
we have no fingernails left as Hayden watches
tensely while his case wobbles and balances precariously on top of a pile of luggage as a tractor-
trailer hauls it across to the waiting plane. We could
hit the stupid innocent bystanders, the stupid
innocent little poodle which dashes out across the
darkened airfield in front of the tractor's wheels,
causing it to swerve . . . and . . . and the case falls . . .
and the catch bursts, and there are two million
dollars swept like snowflakes, like swirling confetti,
in the jet stream of the parked planes in the glare of
the night lights as Hayden watches, impassive.

Kubrick isn't finished with you yet. The money
has gone, but can Hayden and his girl get away
before the two cops standing in the entrance discover who checked in that suitcase? He could get a
taxi. But, as in life, the taxis don't stop: they are all

taken. Someone speaks to the detectives; they move towards him. "Run," says the girl. "You can still get away." But Hayden stands there, hands at his sides. Those massive hands could make mincemeat of the cops, but there he stands, dazed still at the sight of all that money just blowing away. He mutters something. It is inaudible (clever touch, that). And waits to be arrested.

And, you, the audience, stagger out: wrung out by suspense. Not sickened by brutality, not blunted by violence, not torn by sexual symbolism that you may barely understand but that disturbs horribly. You have been thrilled and you have been *entertained*. Superbly.

After *The Killing* Stanley Kubrick made the First World War story, *Paths of Glory*, the spectacular *Spartacus*, and the classics mentioned at the start of this chapter.

With every film he has broadened and deepened his themes, pointed his messages, brought his techniques nearer and nearer to perfection. And, with the new permissive age of the cinema, he has been able to show all the things, in bloody detail, that the young man who made *Killer's Kiss* and *The Killing* cannot have dreamed would be permitted on the screen.

But for me, what he has added in what a lot of clever people call seriousness, he has diminished in entertainment. I make no apology for liking entertainment in the cinema, when made with the brilliance of a Kubrick. I wish that, with all that he has gained from the Seventies, he would make another suspense movie in a direct line of progression from those two classics of the Fifties.

ABOVE LEFT *Sterling Hayden and Marie Windsor in* The Killing *(Harris-Kubrick 1956)*
ABOVE *Kirk Douglas in* Paths of Glory *(Bryna-Harris & Kubrick 1957)*
BELOW *Kirk Douglas again, this time with Jean Simmons in* Spartacus *(Universal-Bryna 1960)*

And Now...

SUSPENSE is a question, and the question now is: "What is happening to suspense films in the Seventies?"

The answer is not a happy one. They are being joked, sexed, bashed and bloodied out of being.

There was a time in the Sixties when the glorious era of the private eye thrillers was succeeded by some very fine spy suspense stories. It was a logical progression: the spy of the screen was very much the same man as the private detective had been. He was a loner; he was a bit of a rebel against established powers but worked for them, chippily, because he believed in a basic right and justice more deeply than his flip wisecracks might have indicated. He regarded the world with a cynical eye, jaundiced by experience, and this was just as well because he was not too surprised when he was double-crossed by everybody.

Probably the best of the field was Martin Ritt's *The Spy Who Came in from the Cold* (1965), scripted by Paul Dehn and Guy Trosper from John Le Carré's novel with a verisimilitude of rare integrity. The unutterable sadness of the characters suffused the film with a tragic melancholy which gave an echoing depth to its tensions – and possibly disappointed less perceptive audiences who did not like seeing their idol Richard Burton as a seedy, weary, worn-out and burnt-out agent.

More colourful, more positive, more exciting (but more superficial) was Ivan Foxwell's production of *The Quiller Memorandum* (1966), with George Segal and Alec Guinness, directed at breathtaking pace by Michael Anderson and with the hallmark of a Harold Pinter screenplay. And a worthy twin to this brought Frank Sinatra to England to make and star in Stanley Mann's screenplay of Francis Clifford's novel, *The Naked Runner* (1967), directed with high-tension excitement by Sidney J. Furie.

The suspense was still strong, the level of excitement high, in the Harry Saltzman productions of Len Deighton's early spy thrillers . . . but was the first small step away from plausibility being taken? A hint of the James Bonds?

Deighton's hero was a new and unglamorous sort of spy who was in the job because it was better than being in jail and paid £30 a week plus expenses (putting in his expenses bothered him, too). In the books he had no name, and I remember the consternation of Bill Canaway, one of the early writers called in by Harry Saltzman, when he realised that he was trying to create a movie around an anonymous man. Bill Canaway gave him the deliberately colourless name of Harry Palmer – and Harry Palmer became, indelibly, Michael Caine in *The Ipcress File*, *Funeral in Berlin* and *Billion Dollar Brain*.

But when Harry Saltzman and Albert R. Broccoli exploded the James Bond thrillers on to the screen, the classic spy suspense story was noisily elbowed aside. The Bond films must have been the most successful series ever made. Their delighted audiences can scarcely be numbered. They are tremendous entertainment. But their sort of spy-catchery has very little to do with suspense.

As the hero has become further removed, not only from life, but also from Ian Fleming's original conception, so the mechanical gimmickry has taken over more and more of the action. The stunt and special effects teams reign supreme. Press a button and, with one bound, Superman of the Seventies is free – to leap into the next frame of a multi-coloured, mechanised, motion picture strip cartoon. Jokey James lives on and suspense is shouted down.

The process was probably taken to its extreme in "lesser Bonds" – things like the U.N.C.L.E. spy series starring Robert Vaughn and David McCallum, or the even less believable Matt Helm series with Dean Martin.

PRECEDING PAGES *The Mafia's way of settling an argument in* The Godfather *(Alfan 1971)*
Three aspects of secret agents;
LEFT *A world-worn Richard Burton in* The Spy Who Came In From The Cold *(Salem 1965)*
ABOVE *Michael Caine trains his gun on Nigel Green and Guy Doleman in* The Ipcress File *(Lowndes/Steven 1965)*
BELOW *Frank Sinatra surrounded by Derren Nesbitt and friends in* The Naked Runner *(Artanis Enterprises 1967)*

If the mechanised jokesters have ousted the private eye and serious spy props of the suspense cinema, what about that other familiar character who was a sturdy peg on which to hang many a thriller – the lone cop? He has attracted some brilliant directors in his time. Otto Preminger, for example, in 1950 with *Where the Sidewalk Ends*. He used a straightforward, powerful storytelling technique, scorning pretentious camera angles and quirky touches of the bizarre in order to root his suspense in realism.

Dana Andrews was the honest, tough New York policeman, always in trouble with his superiors because he liked his own strong-arm methods as much as he detested crooks. He was believable in a way the Bonds and Solos and Helms have never been: when he hit someone, his knuckles hurt. The man he wanted to hit was Gary Merrill, a smooth villain given to sniffing a nasal inhaler between lines. It was Merrill who encapsulated the plot, the setting, and pointed up the title. "Why are you always trying to push me in the gutter?" he asked Andrews. "I have as much right on the sidewalk as you."

Andrews's obsession was rooted in his hidden, shaming knowledge that he was the son of a thief. His fierce hatred of criminals led him to use their own illegal methods to destroy them, and the pursuit of justice became blurred in personal vendetta.

There was a similar ambivalent theme underlying another peak in post-war suspense films: *The Big Heat*, directed by Fritz Lang in 1953. Here the honest cop was Glenn Ford. He was ordered to stop investigating the suicide of a corrupt police officer, but refused. His wife was killed by a bomb meant for him and, spurred now by revenge even more than justice, he resigned from the police force and pursued his enemies with manic determination, gradually becoming as cruel and ruthless as they were.

The film's tensions were strongly enhanced by two intriguing incidentals. One was the presence of Lee Marvin – later to become famous as the toughest of all screen villains – flexing his mayhem muscles by scarring Gloria Grahame's face with a scalding coffee pot. The other was an interesting foreshadowing of *The Godfather* in the characterisation of the chief villain (Alexander Scourby) – a loving family man who at the same time ran a criminal empire with business efficiency.

But the character-dimensions of such films have become superfluous in the Seventies, and the archetypal cop of today is Clint Eastwood in *Dirty Harry* (1971) . . . sullen, boorish, silent with-

BELOW LEFT *Dana Andrews (left) and Gene Tierney in* Where The Sidewalk Ends *(Fox 1950)*
ABOVE LEFT *Glenn Ford stands over Lee Marvin in* The Big Heat *(Columbia 1953)*
Marlon Brando (above) holding court, and Brando's eldest son (below) after his rivals have caught up with him in The Godfather *(Alfan 1971)*

ABOVE *Donald Sutherland in* Klute *(Pakula/Warners 1971), which also starred Jane Fonda*
BELOW *Alec McCowen confronts murder suspect Jon Finch in* Frenzy *(Hitchcock for Universal 1972)*
RIGHT *Frank Sinatra prepares for a "hit" in* The Naked Runner *(Artanis Enterprises 1967)*
OVERLEAF *Burt Reynolds is a busy man in* Shamus *(Columbia/Weitman 1972)*

However, there is hope yet. When it went on general release in Britain in 1973 it was paired with *Klute* (1971) – and there was a film which took advantage of all the relaxed standards governing what can now be shown on the screen, and blended them with sheer suspense in the grand tradition.

Perhaps it is not coincidence that Klute himself (Donald Sutherland) was a mixture of lone cop and private eye: a police officer who was hired privately to investigate somebody's disappearance. The trail led him deep into the world of New York call-girls, pimps and drug addicts. It was all shown unblinkingly, the vice, the degradation, but with intelligent compassion and honest humanity instead of the leer that so often sits on the face of the Seventies. Although scarcely more talkative than Dirty Harry, Klute emerged as a whole human being rather than as a robot programmed to shoot and hit. And as the prostitute Bree Daniel, Jane Fonda achieved a characterisation that has never been surpassed in all the ample literature of tarts with hearts.

Klute was as modern, as honest and unflinching as any fanatic for realism could ask; yet it was never prurient, never needlessly violent, never brutal – and for sheer, entertaining suspense, it was up there with the great ones: an enormous tribute to the producer-director Alan J. Pakula.

Klute was an exception to the sex-and-violence trend of the Seventies. So was Alfred Hitchcock's 1972 thriller, *Frenzy*, scripted by Anthony Schaffer. The old master's first British film since 1950, it was, despite its modishly realistic rape scene,

out apparent reason; incapable equally of thought or of any human feeling; solving all problems with a blast from a revolver so heavy that it takes two hands to aim it. *Dirty Harry* supplanted suspense by action, tension by brutality, character by a bigger and better bullet.

LEFT *Ryan O'Neal takes sensible precautionary measures in* The Thief Who Came to Dinner (*Tandem 1973*)
ABOVE *Vera Clouzet and Yves Montand in Henri-George Clouzet's classic* Wages of Fear (*Filmsonor C1CC-Fona-Roma-Vera Film 1953*)

OVERLEAF *Three more survivors in Alfred Hitchcock's* Lifeboat (*20th Century-Fox 1943*)

strangely old-fashioned and pleasantly workman-like in its techniques. Maximum suspense was squeezed from the sequences where a psychopathic killer (Barry Foster) tried frantically to recover the body of one of his victims (Anna Massey) from its hiding-place in a sack of potatoes in the back of a vegetable lorry hurtling through the night from Covent Garden market: clenched in her rigid fingers was a monogrammed tiepin which could have identified him. And Hitchcock – as always, counterpointing tension with humour – injected some delicious domestic comedy moments when Alec McCowen, as the police inspector, suffered the agonies of the would-be *cordon bleu* cookery imposed upon him with sublime confidence by his wife, Vivien Merchant.

Who, in the show-it-all Seventies, will produce a wordless 30-minute burglary sequence like that which held audiences spellbound with tension when Jules Dassin's *Rififi* came to the screen in 1955? Who will equal the heart-stopping impact of Henri-Georges Clouzot's 1953 prize-winner *The Wages of Fear*? An incredibly simple, modest film, about a group of multi-national down-and-outs driving two trucks loaded with nitro-glycerine through the mountains of Central America, yet one which has never been matched for sustained, unrelenting suspense. I would not swap 11 minutes of that for the famous 11-minute car chase directed with such verve by Peter Yates in the 1968 *Bullitt* – even though it is said that star Steve McQueen scorned to use a double at the wheel.

It often seems that suspense in the classic mould is being drowned in the fashionable flood of sex and brutality, blood and machine-made gimmickry.

But the cinema is a creature of fashions; and fashions, by definition, fade and are supplanted. As the wild rush of "freedom" to the screen subsides, there will be more films which, like *Klute*, take the best of the new liberty and ally it to the most durable of the old disciplines.

The cinema, too, is a medium above all for storytelling: a place where we go to see (to use Hitchcock's words) life with the dull bits cut out.

So long as audiences remain with that desire, it is still too soon in the story of suspense in the cinema for the final titles to roll with the words –

THE END

Acknowledgments

The publishers owe a debt of gratitude to the numerous people and organizations who have helped make this book possible by allowing them the run of their collection of stills and memorabilia and by putting information of one kind or another at their disposal.

The publishers are particularly grateful to the Alan Frank Collection for the provision of stills and invaluable information; to Mr Fred Zentner of The Cinema Bookshop, London; to the staff of all departments of the British Film Institute, the Museum of Modern Art, New York, British Lion Films for the stills from *Don't Look Now* and Twentieth Century-Fox for the stills from *Inferno*. Finally to all those in the film industry without whom this book would have been impossible, goes a special thank you.

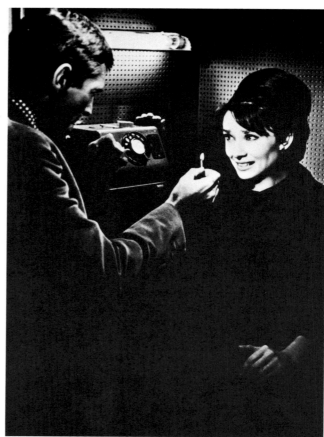

Index of Film Titles

Page numbers in italics refer to illustrations

General Index

Page numbers in italics refer to illustrations

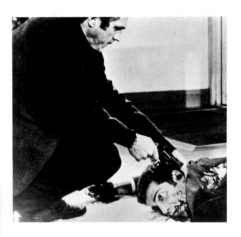

First published 1974 *by Octopus Books Limited,* 59 *Grosvenor Street, London* W1
ISBN 0 7064 0371 1
© 1974 *Octopus Books Limited*
Produced by Mandarin Publishers Limited, 14 *Westlands Road, Quarry Bay, Hong Kong*
Printed in Hong Kong